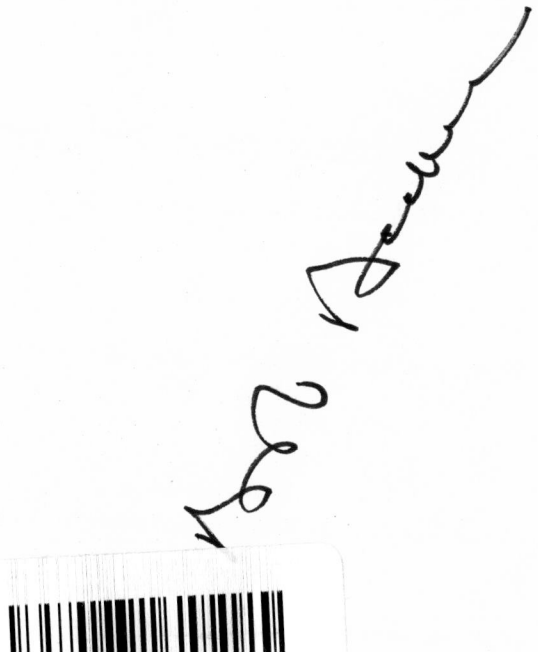

"Chips Off the Ol' Block!"

by Bob Becker

YARD SALE!

*Country Living Sprinkled With Smiles*

**Cover illustrations by Bill Thornley**

Printed 1997
In the United States of America
by White Birch Printing, Inc.
Spooner, Wisconsin 54801

Second Printing, 1998

ISBN 1-885548-04-4

To order, contact:
Boot Prints
701 College St.
Spooner, WI 54801
Phone (715) 635-2317

# Dedication

*In memory of Ted Kemen...*
*my uncle, good friend, and story teller supreme.*

# Foreword

Back in my farm-country boyhood, to be called a "chip off the old block" might be interpreted in two ways. Say I'd done something well, something that emulated a respected grandfather, for instance. If so, an uncle or aunt would speak the words in a complimentary fashion.

But say the opposite occurred. Say I'd displayed a less-than-desirable trait, like a short temper perhaps. If so, I might well have been addressed with a disapproving shake of the head and a reference made to someone known to fly off the handle easily.

The connotation, and its two sides, very likely came from the woodpiles that in by-gone days stood alongside country dwellings. There firewood was manufactured, chunks of oak and maple that were sawn and split down to smaller size for drying and handling.

A good sound chunk would yield good sound smaller pieces ... good "chips" off the block, wood that would burn hot on cold winter nights.

Conversely, a poor chunk, one perhaps that was riddled with punk and rot, would yield poor "chips," wood that would sputter and smoke and yield little in the way of comfort.

In view of the range of personalities in the human race, it's easy to imagine how an analogy emerged between chunks of wood and people, and their mutual characteristics.

I feel indeed fortunate, that in the woodpile of my life, I found a lot of good "blocks," people that I admired and respected ... relatives, teachers, friends. Folks that I would be proud to be called a "chip" off of.

One that bears particular mention is my Uncle Ted, to whom this book is dedicated.

Uncle Ted was a masterful storyteller. His skills I did not recognize as a youngster. But later in life, I sought him out just to listen to him. He could tell a serious tale, but his best were those that had a touch of lightness, a smile in them.

I can see him and hear him yet, as he wove his words, a twinkle in his eyes and a mischievous chuckle in his voice, as if he were letting the listener in on one of the deepest secrets of the world.

I like to believe I gained an appreciation for a good story from Uncle Ted, particularly those with a humorous side to them.

I'd like to believe also, that in a small way, I'm a chip off of him, that he was a block from which my own life took some shape.

The stories that follow are chips of my own. May they, however, meet the standards that my old story-telling mentor would have set for himself.

# Acknowledgements

To properly thank everyone who contributed to this book is difficult to do. Such appreciation, for example, might well be projected back to my boyhood days. To dedicated teachers who taught me to spell and to construct a sentence. And to long-gone relatives who, through their own ethics, influenced my perspectives toward life.

First and foremost, however, my gratitude goes to the many individuals who allowed me to look into their lives, and to write about them. A number of such kind and generous folks are to be found in the tales that follow.

All of the stories appeared originally as weekly newspaper columns from 1986 to 1997. In some instances, time and other circumstances, have altered those settings.

My thanks is also extended to the several newspaper publishers and editors, who along the way saw fit to put my words into print. They've been great to work with and to know.

Lastly, a sincere bow to friends and family members who contributed, sometimes directly, sometimes indirectly. And for their smiles and laughs in response to words I wrote. Special thanks goes to Marian, my wife ... Momma in these stories ... for her criticisms and counsel. Her help was invaluable.

I'm indebted!

The Author

# Contents

# Grandma's Kitchen

Apple pies steaming, sending their sweet aroma throughout the house, cooling on a pantry shelf. Loaves of golden-brown bread, freshly baked, resting on a white dish towel. The soft rumble of a rolling pin flattening cookie dough before my grandmother's hands.

Ah, yes! The sights, the smells, the sounds of old-fashioned farm kitchens. What a wonderful world they were!

Thanksgiving Day is fast-approaching. Thanksgiving Day generates thoughts of the old-time farm kitchens I once knew. A time before electricity-powered mixers, and switch-turned-on ovens. A time before pre-packaged pie crusts, pre-peeled potatoes, and pre-prepared gravy.

Now those days weren't necessarily better, just different, part of a long-gone era of American culture. I'm sure that the mother, grandmothers and aunts that I knew then would have gladly traded their old-style kitchens for the modern ones we know today.

Still, those long ago kitchens had a charm I find, as I look back to my boyhood. Those old kitchens were actually mini-factories, places where raw materials arrived to be manufactured into useful products, things on which families depended. Flour, for instance, came in fifty-pound bags. In time and with skilled hands, it became bread for the table. And the white cloth bags that it came in were made into pillow cases, aprons, and petticoats.

Dominating the old kitchen scenes were the big wood-burning ranges, with their black stove lids, warming ovens and reservoirs where a supply of hot water could always be found. Except perhaps on the coldest of winter mornings, when the dipper would be frozen tight in the water pail over by the sink.

Over those old cook stoves, farm wives hovered, performing magic literally as they turned out scrumptious meals. Three times a day, seven days a week, all year long.

Long wooden tables occupied the centers of the rooms. Covered with oilcloth, they served a multitude of purposes, all the way from the meals that were served on them, to the Sunday afternoon card games that were played when the big-city relatives came for a visit.

I can see my grandmother still, as she sat at the end of her kitchen table, peeling apples from her orchard, long red ribbons of apple skins flowing before her paring knife. And kneading bread. How she could knead bread dough!

"Making bread," as she called it, was a science in itself. The night before she'd mix a cake of yeast with potato water, add flour, her other secret ingredients, and set it all in a big pan behind her wood-fired range for the night.

The next day the white dough would be overflowing the pan's rim. On the flour-dusted kitchen table she'd dump the white mass. And with a vengeance, she'd attack, beating, slamming, punching, rolling that dough into loaf sizes, plopping them into bread pans and into her oven.

It was there on that table that the chickens, ducks and geese came to be dipped into scalding-hot water and wrapped with old newspapers. It was there that I got my first lessons in plucking feathers, watching as the down from the ducks and geese was carefully saved to make the softest of pillows and the warmest of feather ticks, comforters under which I snuggled many a winter night in a cold upstairs bedroom.

Too, old kitchens were family-gathering centers. Quiet, not like my kitchen of today which resounds to buzzers and bells and fans. No, there grandfather sat in the evenings after the chores were done, in his high-backed rocking chair, toasting his shins to the heat radiating from the dying coals of grandma's cook stove fire. There he sat, smoking his corncob pipe, reading the weekly paper, the only sounds coming from the snap of the fire, the sputter of the gas light overhead, and the crinkle of a page of his paper being turned.

Nearby, again at the end of her kitchen table, grandma sat, busy darning socks and sewing patches on overalls. Perhaps an uncle would come down from the attic with a couple of ears of popcorn he'd raised, to be shelled and popped in a big black skillet, a special treat to a young country bumpkin.

Somewhere I hope there's one of those old-time country kitchens preserved for posterity. With a long-handled black coffee grinder, a red-striped roller towel, and a cumbersome wooden telephone hanging from its walls. With blue denim barn jackets hanging from pegs and four-buckle overshoes standing in a corner. And a big open-mouthed green wood box, like the one I was expected to fill each day.

They don't make kitchens like that any more.

November, 1994

# On The Rummage Sale Trail

Well, another season has ended, and it's a sad day. No more early morning sunrises; no more creeping out of town on sleepy streets; no more the thrill of the chase; no more bragging-size beauties from the car trunk. It's a sad time, a time for reflection back to the season opener last spring.

No, I'm not talking about the trout season. I'm talking about the rummage sale season.

Momma's had a good year. She bagged some real good catches, some fine trophies.

Take those three washboards for instance, that are mounted on the laundry room wall over her washer and dryer. You know, the kind Grandma used fifty years ago to scrub overalls and longjohns before electricity came to the back country.

There's a National and a Maid-Rite and a third of unknown breed. Critters from ancient times that have lost the battle of evolution and gone into extinction with the passenger pigeon. Only through the efforts of dedicated conservationists like Momma will these once-proud species be preserved for future generations to know.

It's always a joy to watch the season unfold. There are the phone calls to partners the night before and the huddles in the kitchen to plot strategy. Maps are drawn and plans made with a precision that would make the average deer camp blush with shame.

Opening hours and regulations are checked and re-checked. Where are bargain populations the highest? Should new territory be explored before the hunt? What methods should be used? Solitary still hunts or should a drive be made? Every hunter knows you have to know the habitat.

And all the work pays off.

In a corner of the kitchen stands a stone crock, a fair trophy in itself; one you just don't bag every day. But in the crock are nine rolling pins, all neatly cleaned and refurbished, standing tall. Each a tender reminder of a successful stalk as the sun peeked rose-colored from the east.

Ah, yes! Nine rolling pins. A very good catch. It's nice to have a supply on hand. One never knows when one will blow a gasket or burn out a bearing. They have a habit of doing that you know just after the 50,000 mile warranty runs out. And parts are slow to get, especially for those foreign jobs.

In another nook sits a second crock. Nestled in it are five of the rarest of specimens, three eggbeaters and two potato mashers. Momma looks at them with feelings so deep, so strong, that at times a tear curls gently down her cheek.

How can anyone appreciate; how can anyone understand the thrill, the satisfaction of tracking an eight-point potato masher as dawn is breaking and bagging it as it rests under a card table in the far corner of a garage?

Then there's the "catch and release" ethic. Muskie fishermen think they invented it. Not true. Not so. Rummage sale ladies were practicing catch and release long before fishermen copied it.

It works this way. The daily bag is carefully examined and handled to assure there are no injuries. The catch is then cached in a safe place, and then the next year Momma holds her very own sale. All the little critters are again released into the wild so that the resource can be enjoyed once more by all. It's a lofty, noble ethic that other sports might well heed.

But most of all, I like the way Momma remembers me when she's out hunting. Sure over the years I've brought her a bouquet or two of pussy willows and a chunk or two of exquisite driftwood from my fishing and hunting excursions. But those little trinkets pale in the face of the three washtubs that she brought home and handed to me with love welling up in her eyes. I'm still choked up!

Yes, the season's over, and it'll be a long winter; a long time before the little cardboard signs show up again along country roads. A winter of memories of the big ones that got away, of the fellowship of good companions. A winter of longing and dreaming of a spring to come.

I know how she feels. The trout season just closed.

October, 1986

# Sweet Maple Syrup

A labor of love!

The tinge of blue-grey wood smoke sifting softly through the trees caught my eye. The property was my neighbor's and somebody had a fire going back in there. What was going on? I stopped the pickup and followed the trail in the snow back through the hardwoods.

And there I found Dale Reinhart huddled over an open fire cooking. Cooking maple sap, that is. That was two years ago, and each spring now I stop for a visit.

Such was the case the other day. The woods was peaceful; spring was in the air, the sunshine warming my back through my jacket. A couple of crows cawed; the staccato sound of a woodpecker hammering echoed in the distance. Chickadees flitted and chirped around me as I walked the winding trail through the big maples, basswoods and birches.

The wood smoke and white steam curling skyward ahead told me he was there. But I could see as I approached that he'd "modernized." A little shelter had been built. There'd be no more huddling under a wind-toppled basswood to get out of the rain. No longer was there an open fire. Two stoves made from steel barrels were snapping and crackling, and a big kettle and a large flat pan both filled with maple sap were bubbling merrily. Steam wafted through the shelter as the water boiled away. I'd found Dale working on his first batch of maple syrup.

Now, the making of maple syrup is a good-sized industry here in our state. Wisconsin is one of the leading producers in the nation. Producers come in all sizes from small to big.

But what I like about Dale Reinhart's operation is that it's strictly personal; a labor of love; syrup for his own use; something that he enjoys doing very much. For six springs now he's been doing it. He told me he spends three to four weeks tapping trees, collecting sap, boiling it down. And from that he'll end up with about twenty-five quarts of syrup.

And he showed me how it's done. White plastic pails hung from the maple trunks. Knowing maple trees is of course, the first secret; and he laughed as he pointed to a basswood that he'd once tapped. "Nothing came out!" he explained.

The hard, or sugar maple, is the best species. But any member of the maple family will do, and he had buckets hanging on several big soft, or red, maples.

After a tree is tapped by drilling a hole into the outer wood, a spigot or "spile" is inserted to catch and drain the sap. Most spiles are made of steel but Dale makes his own from sumac wood. A four-inch piece is cut, and the soft center pith is pushed out to form a short wooden pipe. Indians and pioneers used the same method many years ago.

Once the sap is collected, the hard work of boiling it down begins. About 12 to 15 gallons of sap are needed to produce a quart of syrup, and the boiling requires a watchful eye.

Periodically he dipped a thermometer into the boiling sap. The temperature was holding at 212°, the boiling point for water. But, as he explained, when it rises above that, the sap

*Dale Reinhart boils maple sap into syrup.*

is approaching syrup consistency. The magic figure is 219°. If the mixture is allowed to go beyond that, it will flare into a granulated "sand" or sugar; and a whole day's work is wasted.

So when the condensed sap approaches 219°, he quits for the day. The mixture is drained off to be taken home where he and his wife can finish it off under more controlled conditions.

Finally the syrup is filtered to remove impurities, bottled and stored to await breakfasts of pancakes and waffles.

Wouldn't it be easier to buy a couple gallons I suggested. He laughed and said, "A guy has to be a little crazy to be out here all day for a couple quarts of syrup. But I enjoy this. I'm perfectly content to be out here all day."

And I can understand that. It's a great way to say good-bye to winter, hello to spring. There's the fresh air and Mother Nature coming alive. There are tired muscles and deep, restful sleeps at night.

Then there are the amber bottles of maple syrup to touch it all off. And how sweet it all is!

March, 1987

# Momma And The Love Birds

Momma's got a big problem on her hands, and I don't know how to help her. Over the years, she's been a first-class mother and mother-in-law. But now she's facing a new and different challenge.

There's this pair of robins you see, that have taken up house-keeping in the yew bush outside the bedroom window. Now Momma's all in favor of that, but she's having a tough time dealing with the life style of two young love birds just starting out in life.

There's that wacko, shiftless husband robin for instance. For two weeks all he did was flit around all night only to come home at daybreak so bleary-eyed that he couldn't tell the difference between his own reflection in the bedroom window and a rival robin. So he'd bang his head against the window for a couple hours every morning until he got the cobwebs cleared out.

Now, how could a sweet young robin wife ever get mixed up with a bird brain like that? But she did.

And then the eggs began to appear. First one, then two, three and finally four. Momma just shook her head. Such a goings-on! Don't these young robin kids know how much work goes into raising a family?

Momma checked the nest every day. Often the sweet young thing wasn't around. Momma would come in the front door muttering, "Where's that bird? Doesn't she know those eggs are getting cold? She'd better get with it if she expects to raise a family!"

Well, the other day I was cutting the lawn so I decided to take a peek myself. Sure enough, there they were; four little helpless naked bodies huddled together.

When I told Momma, she exclaimed, "Four! You mean all four eggs hatched! It's just like that pair to have quadruplets the first year!"

So she went out and took a look for herself. "The nest's too small!" she said. "How in the world will that young mother be able to bring up four kids in a house that will barely hold two?"

I just stood back watching and listening to the whole thing.

It was then that the sweet young thing appeared with a flourish of her tail feathers in the oak tree above Momma's head.

Momma looked up and began to give the young mother a lecture on the responsibilities of parenthood. Well, I want to tell you there were some sharp words exchanged between the two. I couldn't understand exactly what the sweet young thing was saying, but I'm sure it was unprintable.

Finally things settled down, but Momma still wasn't done.

"Where's that good-for-nothing mate of hers? All he does all day is hang around the bird bath with that flashy oriole. Why isn't he out bringing home the worm-and-bug bacon to feed those four babies?" she snorted.

Well, it isn't hard to see where I stand in this whole family squabble. I'm just an innocent bystander. I try to tell Momma that times have changed; that young bird folks are different these days; that it's none of our business how that robin couple chooses to live.

But knowing Momma, I doubt that I'm getting through. She'll be out there every day checking and disapproving of what's going on. And I'm certain that there will be more sharp words between her and the sweet young thing.

But I think Momma might be on to something. Right now she's looking for an ornithologist that can translate Dr. Spock into bird language. If she can pull that off; maybe, just maybe, things will work out between the two of them.

I sure hope so. I hate family fights.

June, 1986

# Omar, You Blew It!

March is a dippy month.

I was born in March. Perhaps that explains some things about the month, or me, depending on how you look at it.

As I write, bearing down on us outside is what the weather people call "a major winter storm."

Oh, the TV guys let me know. "A powerful low pressure system is organizing in the Rockies," they say; all very professional. Maybe a foot of snow, they tell. But knowing March, by the time this hits the papers, the white stuff could well be rolling down the rivers. That's March.

I say March is a dippy month because a lot of things are wrong with March.

First of all, March is too long. March is a draggy month. something went wrong, and I'm pretty sure I know what, when March was laid out.

The way I figure it, an ancient Egyptian, Omar the astronomer, was sitting on top of a pyramid one night several thousand years ago, studying the stars, working on a calendar. My guess is that old Omar had a jug of homebrew fig juice with him.

How else can you explain it? Here we sit with a March that's 31 days long. And February gets only 28. Something tilted the telescope.

I say take a day or two off March and give it to February.

We'd all come out better.

We'd help February. February's too short. Look at all the holidays in February. Put another holiday or two in February, and we won't get any mail all month.

Besides, if February had a couple more days, we ice fishermen could get more time to fish for northerns and walleyes before the season closes March first. That's good reason enough to change the calendar.

Shorten up March and April would get here sooner. Everyone knows April is a spring month. Nobody cares if it snows in April. We all laugh at April snowstorms. We smile at the neighbors as we shovel the sidewalks and happily say, "It won't last!"

Think about it. Think of all the good psychological value we'd gain if April came sooner.

Stories in the papers about the first robin and the baseball season starting would be out earlier. Ladies could dream about planting their petunias. Tickets for "ice out" contests would sell like hotcakes. We could celebrate April Fool's Day earlier. And we'd all be uplifted.

Back to dippy March.

It comes in like a lion or a lamb and goes out like a lion or a lamb, they say. Everything hinges on the first couple days of the month. Get some cold or snow at the start of the month, and we're guaranteed to bask in balmy sunshine at the end. Now that's real scientific. My Egyptian friend, Omar, must have figured that out the same night he gave March too many days.

I can see him now, teetering on the tip of that pyramid, his juice gourd overflowing, looking down through bleary eyes at a mangy yellow tom cat prowling below. "Looks like a lion to me down there! Must be time for March!" he probably thought. Thanks a lot, Omar!

Then there's St. Patrick's Day, the day long ago when Old Pat chased the snakes out of Ireland. Maybe. I'm suspicious. The only snakes I've ever heard about in the middle of March have been the snow snakes certain bluegill fishermen have been known to see when the fishing's slow and the refreshments flow.

We pay tribute to Old Pat by running around with green clover leaves pinned on our pockets and drinking green beverages. Green? What's green in March?

And the first day of Spring, March 20. So what if the sun is directly over the equator that day. If we're lucky, the sugar maple sap will be barely dripping into Rollie Schaefer's buckets down at Shell Lake.

Having had some experience with bureaucracies, I suppose it's asking too much to change March. I expect I'll just have to live with March, dippy as it is. After all, look what happened to the metric system.

So let 'er snow, and let 'er blow. Momma's got the pantry well-stocked, the snowblower's running good, and there's two weeks firewood in the basement. Besides, the moisture will help the farmers and cut the fire season.

But Omar -- I still say you blew it, old buddy.

March, 1989

# Boys Of Winters Past

Boys of winter, I came to call them. Two sixty-something guys on cross-country skis, retracing the paths of their pasts. And for a few hours, savoring treasured boyhood memories.

"Remember now, no more than twenty-five miles an hour," I'd said to the pair; Zino Tully, my next door neighbor, and his life-long friend, John Hovey, from out west of town a few miles. The two were clamping on their skis, preparing to escort me back to Rumpskinner, Big and Little Izzy, and Tea Kettle; hills where, as youngsters, they'd spent many a Saturday afternoon fifty years ago, in 1930 times.

As I plodded along on my snowshoes, I watched with envy, as the two smoothly and effortlessly out-distanced me; their skis hissing, slicing through the packed, crusted snow.

For they were skiers back then... in those long-ago times. And they're skiers still.

"I ski about five to six miles a day, three times a week," Hovey told me. "I can ski right out my back door onto Washburn County Forest lands."

And Tully, who plans to once more ski in this year's Birkebeiner, added, "I do ten kilometers, about five to six miles, four or five days a week."

Their expertise showed as they led me through Tony Lombard's pasture; hilly land, sprinkled with mammoth old oak trees.

And there, at the base of a steep, westward-facing slope, they paused to wait for me.

"This is the hill we called Rumpskinner," Tully said. "I first came here when I was eight years old. From a distance it doesn't look very big, but when you're at the bottom and look up, it's pretty good-sized."

"Over there, that's Tea Kettle," Hovey added, pointing. "It got its name from the bowl in its center. That was our socializing spot. We'd come out here on bright moon-lit nights to ski and toboggan. We'd build a big bonfire for warmth, and roast hot dogs and marshmallows."

As I caught the nostalgia of the moment, I envied them. Two senior citizens returning to the scene of their youth, to ski. And there was their world, just as they'd left it some fifty years ago. Not many people can do that, I thought.

"Over there, in that woods, are the Big and Little Izzy hills," they continued. "They were part of the Isabella farm."

"They were the ultimate test of our courage or foolhardiness," said John, "depending on your point of view. The tricky part of Big Izzy was that, instead of leveling out at the bottom, the run made an immediate transition up Little Izzy. The "G" forces were too much for many skiers, and they did spectacular cartwheels up Little Izzy!"

On weekend afternoons, fifty or more kids would be on the hills. "We'd walk out from town along an old cattle lane. There'd be some grown-ups too. Some of our teachers would ski out here," they said.

How did the kids dress, I asked. That brought some smiles. "Most of us wore corduroy breeches and 'high-cuts', high-topped leather boots. And if you didn't have a pair with a jackknife pocket on the side, you were nothing!" Zino said.

"And black corduroy coats with collars and linings of

*John Hovey and Zino Tully ready themselves for a run down Rumpskinner Hill.*

sheepskin," John continued. "On our heads, we wore those old-fashioned leather 'helmets' with straps that buckled under your chin."

And girls? There were lots of girls, they said. "Some were kind of tom-boys. They wore snow pants and suspenders, and long coats. You didn't see the sport-type jackets back then."

Skis were crude by modern standards.

"Most of ours were made of ash or hickory," Hovey recalled, "and sold at Chapman's Hardware store. They came with a toe strap, enough to get a beginner started. But we made rudimentary bindings out of rubber rings from inner tubes, which we'd place over our ankles, then stretch over our toes."

"I used to make bindings out of screen door springs," said Tully.

And the times, what were they like?

"You think back," Zino answered, "and you heard how tough things were in the Depression. But there were a lot of good things too. It didn't seem all that bad because you didn't know any better."

I sat under a gnarled white oak that day, up at the top of Rumpskinner hill, with the wind blowing around me. And I listened, and I watched the faces of the two, as they reminisced.

They'd carried something away from those white slopes some fifty years ago, I decided; something priceless and fulfilling and enduring, something irreplaceable.

Surely, they were boys of winter.

February, 1992

# Fall, The Earth Rests

Fall, the glory time! The earth rests after a hard summer's work.

You can feel it in the subtle change in the wind out of the north as it drifts in off Lake Superior. No longer does it have that soft, gentle, cool caress. Now there's a touch of power in it; and a primeval instinct in us stirs, warning that it's time to get moving. The hazy, lazy days of summer are over.

And you can sense it in the deeper azure blue of the sky and the warm, no longer hot, rays of the sun. One side of me basks while my shade side feels good in a wool shirt.

The roadsides and abandoned clearings are splotched with the colors of late summer wildflowers. As if some mad painter has thrown his brushes at the countryside.

Yellow goldenrod and brown-eyed susans, white daisies, red-headed clover. Purple-blossomed milkweed tipped with orange monarch butterflies on their southward migration.

It's only a matter of a few weeks and the hardwood ridges of aspen, maple and oak will be ablaze with scarlet and gold. Enjoy it, because there'll come a rainy afternoon when the radiance will be swept before the wind, and only bare branches will remain.

The farmer, one eye on the weather, rushes to get his crops in. He doesn't need rain now. There's a silo to be filled and maybe a third crop of alfalfa to put up. A couple killing frosts whiten rooftops at sunrise, and there is corn to be picked and soybeans to be combined.

Red school bus lights flash again on country roads.

Widllife goes on a frenzy of feeding to lay up fat reserves for what they know lies ahead. Wild geese; Canadas, snows, and blues; ride a cold front overhead, shrilly yakking to each other in "V" formations, toward their wintering marshes.

Waters cool; fish shake their summer lethargy and prey on forage fish in earnest, building heavy spawn sacs for their rebirth ritual come spring again.

September, October; my favorite times of the year. But so much to do, and so little time to do it. I hate to see a single day pass.

It's the time of the hunter. In my youth, I counted the days to the hunting season openers. Shotguns and rifles were oiled and re-oiled, and ammunition fondly tucked into shell loops of a battered hunting coat.

The old hunting instinct is still alive. The old double-barrelled twelve gauge will come out of its case and loaded with 7 1/2's for quiet walks on woods trails for partridge. There was a time when I could take five days of timber cruising and then go out and put on a half-dozen miles on weekends for ruffed grouse. But not any more. The rubber bands in the legs don't snap back as fast as they used to. So I'll pace myself.

And a little twenty-two will be packed with long rifles, and I'll plunk myself down on my deer stands to wait out a couple squirrels. They have to be there. They're all around me, teasing, during deer season. I'll find out in a hurry if my eyes need testing.

Then there will be the hard choices. The gun or the fishing rod?

I made the mistake a few years ago of reading a couple articles about fall fishing. Hunting had always been my bag. But I gave the fishing a try, and now I'm hooked on it.

The walleyes have been aceing me out real good the past year. There's a score to be settled! So I'll be out there soaking up the afternoon sunshine and working a jig-and-minnow combination along the weedlines. Don't try it; you might like it too much and like me, you'll have hard decisions to make.

Fall, the glory time! If there was just some way to add a month on each side of it.

But then, there would be just that many more hard choices.

September, 1986

# Long Live Longjohns

You say you've got the winter blues? That the walls are creeping closer? There's a lot of that going around these days.

Turn up the lights, the experts say. Get some exercise, some fresh air. That's how to cope, they say.

Hah! There's more to it than that!

The real problem, I say, is underwear. That's right, our underwear. Longjohns, or the lack thereof, to be exact. Bring back longjohns, I say, and our winter worries would shrink.

Having had a close association (pardon the pun) with longjohns for nigh on to seventy years now, I feel that I speak with a good deal of credibility. Very frankly, and with all modesty, I consider myself one of the world's leading authorities on longjohns. Let's just say I know longjohns from the bottom up!

Please note that I claim to be only one authority. I am fully aware that there are other folks out there who've also researched longjohns. Later, I'll expand on some of their findings.

Above all, I do not want to get into a flap... to be told to button up. I have no intention of pulling the wool over their eyes.

Allow me to bare a few facts about longjohns.

Longjohns come in two styles, one-piece and two-piece. The one-piece go back a long time, probably to the caveman days. The two-piece came out maybe thirty years or so ago. I've worn both. Each has advantages. For example, say you're bending over an ice-fishing tip-up, getting ready to hook a nice northern. The one-piece won't come apart in the middle of your back, exposing your kidneys to a frigid north wind.

The two-piece, on the other hand, are more versatile. Like say your wife wants to go to a football game on a cool October evening. You can always loan her your bottoms.

Longjohns come in a range of fabrics... wool, cotton and synthetics. My research has shown that wool, while it may be a ticklish subject to some, is the warmest. But then, maybe I've only scratched the surface.

All are tricky to launder... without shrinking. I look like a snake getting ready to shed its skin in one of mine! Laundering brings to mind old memories of white one-piece jobs hanging in the winter air on my mother's clothes line years ago, frozen stiffer than a sheet of plywood.

Which brings me to other longjohn experts I've known.

Over the years, I've watched several in action around ice fishing and deer hunting camps. I'll tell you, it's a sight to see... droopy drawers waddling around whipping up a batch of ham hocks and sauerkraut for supper, or bacon and eggs for breakfast. I'll tell you, it's something when burning toast smells better than the cook!

Some of my best information on the rich heritage of longjohns, however, came from an old logger... Skidder Windjammer.

I bumped into old Skid one cold morning many years ago. There he was, standing over a big yellow birch log that he and Bessy, his faithful old mare, had just pulled into a landing. There he stood, his wool shirt half open to his belly button, his longjohns steaming in the winter air.

"Good day for the longjohns, eh Skid?" I said.

"You betcha, Beckee boy," he answered. Old Skid never was much for proper names.

"Yessiree! My daddy wore longjohns and my granddaddy wore longjohns," he went on. "Yep, come the first snow in November, grandma would sew granddaddy into his, and she didn't cut him loose until the frost came out of the tater patch in April!

"Yessiree! Granddaddy would go off to the logging camp and wear that union suit all winter," Skid continued.

"Wouldn't he get a little, shall we say, on the ripe side?" I asked, trying to be as delicate as possible.

"Oh, shore!" Skid answered. "But when camp shut down at spring break-up, granddaddy always did a little of that ill-lee-gal beaver trapping. Always fell through the ice a couple times. That kind of evened him out."

"I see," I replied.

"Yep, shore was hard on the beavers though," Skid chuckled. "Killed a couple of colonies colder than a left-handed monkey wrench! Those conservation guys came out and blamed it on some kind of a dee-seese. Twarn't no dee-seese no how. Twarn't nothing but granddaddy's undies!"

And with that ol' Skid slapped Bessy on the rump, and the two headed back into the woods.

"Stop by again, Beckee boy!" he hollered. "And I'll tell you about my daddy making a walleye trap out of his long-handles. Yessiree, poisoned the Flambeau clean down to Ox Bow!"

There you have it, folks! Some of the more secret intimate undertones of my extensive research on longjohns.

A longjohn worn is a winter scorned, I've always said.

(I've been just itching to tell this story!)

February, 1997

# Hallowed History

It's one of my favorite places. Yet it's just a few miles from my front door. I'm talking about the old portage trail between the Brule River and Lake St. Croix northeast of Solon Springs.

You've never heard of it? I'm not surprised. Mention it to people, and that's the response I usually get.

I like old Wisconsin history. I like the nostalgia, the color, the romance of our early days. I like to stand where history was made. That's why I like the Brule-St. Croix Portage Trail.

If you're familiar with canoe travel, then you know that a portage is a short stretch of high land that separates two bodies of water, either rivers or lakes.

There are many such areas, portages, around the upper midwest. But none can compare with the one between the Brule and the St. Croix Rivers. I know of none that has had more impact on the history of this region. With the coming of the white man in the late 1600's, the old path felt the moccasins and boots of explorers, fur traders, voyageurs and missionaries.

I first walked the old trail some twenty years ago, and an unforgettable experience it was. I walked it again recently with Chuck Zosel, the superintendent of the Brule River State Forest, whose job it is to look after this hallowed piece of heritage.

We walked and we talked; talked about the old diaries and journals kept by explorers who passed that way a hundred, two hundred years ago. How they came up the rapids of the St. Mary's River where the Sault Ste. Marie locks now stand at the east end of Lake Superior. And finally how they made their way to the Brule River to pole their birch bark and dugout canoes up to its head.

And there at the headwaters, the two-mile portage began; a footpath through the pine woods to the upper end of Lake St. Croix. Then southward down the St. Croix River and into the Mississippi watershed those voyageurs travelled.

Travel went both ways. In his book, "The Brule River of Wisconsin," Leigh P. Jerrard states: "It may have been used every year for well over one hundred fifty years and it is not improbable that in the aggregate, there were thousands of trips by individual traders, voyageurs, missionaries, hunters and explorers up and down this turbulent stream."

Then there's another side of the old trail that I appreciate. Somewhere along it, a place imperceptible to the eye, there's a point in the spruce, cedar and balsam fir-forested bog where the waters divide. A tiny seep-like trickle of water moves northward to mark the beginning of the Brule River; water that flows into Lake Superior, down the Great Lakes, out the St. Lawrence River, and finally into the Atlantic Ocean.

Then there's another little trickle of water that begins a southward journey in the opposite direction. Into Lake St. Croix, down the St. Croix River, into the Mississippi and on to the Gulf of Mexico.

I like places like that. They're special places for me, places with "hands-on" geography and history. Places that I

*Early explorers travelled the Brule-St. Croix River Trail.*

can touch with my feet, see with my eyes.

Yes, Chuck Zosel and I hiked the old portage. We walked and we talked. And we paused at the bronze tablets on the granite stones that tell how people like Michael Curot passed that way back in 1803; Jean Baptiste Cadotte in 1819; Henry R. Schoolcraft in 1820; Nicholas and Joseph Lucius in 1886.

But I also paused to stand beneath the tall Norway pines and once again let my imagination roll. I could see bearded fur traders and their Indian guides struggling along the old trail with battered birch bark canoes and packsacks heavy with beaver hides on their shoulders. I could see black-robed missionaries with gold crosses and chains dangling from their necks. And I could hear the jabber of three languages; French, Chippewa and English.

You say you're looking for something to do with the kids someday? Take a ride to Solon Springs and look up the old trail.

Take a hike on it. It's not necessary to walk the full two miles. Let the kids see and feel where American history was made. Let them sit quietly on the roots of a tall pine tree.

And let them find some roots of their own.

July, 1987

# A Christmas Story

If a merry twinkle in an eye, and a jolly lilt to a voice, are traits for a good Santa Claus, then Elgie McDonough would make a great one.

And if a warm, loving smile is an attribute for Mrs. Claus, then Iona, Elgie's wife, certainly qualifies.

I can see the two now, getting ready for Christmas Eve up at their North Pole home; Elgie hitching the reindeer to his sleigh; Iona busily supervising the elves with last minute toy-making, serving up tasty home-baked Christmas cookies for their coffee breaks.

Close friends, Momma and I spent some time recently visiting with Elgie and Iona at their Barron home; reminiscing about Christmases past, among other things. Elgie'll be 81, Iona 75, come early January. And the two shared some wonderful Christmas memories with us.

"As a little kid, we always seemed to have lots of snow," Elgie mused. "Farm families didn't get their roads plowed, so we went by horses. Dad hitched up Bird and Wilbur to a sled, which had four-foot high sideboards, and spread straw on the bottom. Then he'd pitch in some heavy horse blankets to keep us warm."

And the family would be on its way to a Christmas program at their country school, the main social event of the year for the community.

"Dad would yell 'giddy-up', and away we went. The sleigh bells on the horses, and their heel chains, would jingle, and the steel sled runners squeal as they slid along," Elgie continued. "Along the way, we'd pick up neighbors, sing, and have a jolly good time."

Arriving at the school, the horses would be tied and blanketed, and the program would begin.

"The teacher saw to it that all of the kids, all eight grades, had a part. When it was over, the big fat jolly man with the long white beard and mustasche would come charging in. Santa would call out the names, and the presents handed out; along with candy, peanuts and apples. The Christmas season had begun."

Iona too, has some special childhood memories of Christmas. One of ten children, she remembers Christmases being celebrated in very modest ways back in those early 1920 times. "My oldest brother worked at the Ford Company's plant at Iron Mountain, Michigan, and he always sent a box of gifts home for us kids," she said.

Then, a neighbor who lived nearby also added some special cheer. "She was a jolly, roly-poly person," Iona recalled. "Each year, when it was getting close to Christmas, we'd hear some jingling outside. We'd open the door, and there she'd be, dressed as Santa."

Married in 1936, the McDonoughs farmed and raised turkeys until their retirement several years ago. Through those years, they were active in community affairs. Each year Elgie helped to organize Christmas programs at their church and school. "We'd hold basket socials and pie socials each fall to raise money for Christmas treats for the kids," Elgie said.

And they recall Christmases with their own three youngsters; Karen, Wendell, and Randy. "One year I made a toy tractor for Wendell," Elgie said. I painted it orange just like the Allis Chalmers tractor we had on the farm. He rode it all around the house and the yard!"

Since those early days, their family has grown to include seven grandchildren and two great-grandchildren. "And there's three more on the way," Iona added. As many as can will be home to spend Christmas this year with dad and mom, grandpa and grandma.

Still, there's another side of the McDonoughs' lives. In recent years Elgie has chosen to write poetry, coming to be known as "The Old Country Poet." In 1987, he published a book of his works titled POEMS N' STUFF.

In it are these verses, beautiful lines that fit this Christmas season, called "The Greatest Story".

"The shepherds heard the angels singing
  Around a manger far away
Heralding a newborn baby
  Lying there upon the hay.
The wise men came and brought Him presents
  A star shone brightly up above
The world would change because this infant
  Brought a wondrous kind of love.
So we trim the trees with tinsel
  Greet each person young and old
Sing the Christmas songs that echo
  The greatest story ever told."

December, 1991

# Winter Wimps Out!

Hey, Old Man! What is it with you? What's the program? Winter used to be a respected name in these parts.

Here we are running around on bare roads; the snow plows are gathering rust over at the county shops; and I know a guy who bought a new snowblower last fall that hasn't been out of his garage. I haven't been up on my roof to push the snow off, and there hasn't been a single case of cabin fever reported yet.

There's barely a dent in my woodpile; the neighbors are all kidding me. And the farmers are spreading manure on their fields, laughing in your face. Come on! You've never been one to take that kind of treatment, old chum.

We've been friends a long time, you and I. There's a lot of things I like about you. I've given you your due respect and yes, even fear at times. But this year you haven't got it. You're a pussycat, a patsy.

Oh, sure! Tell me you tried. Tell me how you put good ice on the lakes by the middle of November for us ice fishermen. But what else have you got to brag about? That measly six inches of snow in the woods or a couple of wimpy twenty below nights? Tell me about it.

You used to be a tough old buzzard. People used to talk about bad winters, long winters, cold winters, rough winters. Not now.

You've got us all confused. People go around smirking up their sleeves at the snowbirds that went south to high-priced condos; yet complain that they can't ride their snowmobiles.

Even the wild things. The deer should be holed up in a cedar swamp somewhere battling to stay alive. Not so this year. They're wandering around the country-side enjoying the scenery. And Art Oehmcke and I saw a raccoon strolling in a maple swamp the other day when we were out to Clam Lake ice fishing. Then John Plenke and I saw a bald eagle sitting on the ice of a cranberry marsh soaking up sunshine one afternoon. Have you no pride in your reputation, old buddy?

And don't tell me you're sorry. I've known you too long. You're not that kind of a guy. You've always been more like the grade school bully, the bimbo who's nice as pie to you one day and then beats your brains out the next.

I have to warn you, old friend. You're slipping fast, real fast. You better get moving and in a hurry.

You see, one of these days that sweet little sultry southern siren, Ms. Spring, is going to come waltzing into town. She'll be wearing one of those flimsy, peek-a-boo blouses and a big white wide-brimmed hat with yellow daffodils sticking up. Her dark eyes will be a-flashing and her long eye lashes a-fluttering, ala Scarlet O'Hara style.

There'll be a perfume scented with magnolia blossoms trailing her; and she'll look at us and say something like, "Well, I do declare! It shonuff is mighty fine to see all you nice Yankee folks again, y'all!"

Oh, we know she's fickle, a little balmy in her barometer. But folks are going to throw their arms around her and hug her and kiss her like a long-lost rich aunt.

Now I know, old chum, that you've always thought she

was a cheap hussy. You two never did get along. I expect there will be the usual cussing and kicking and scratching going on between you two. It happens every year.

But let me give you a little advice, friend to friend. You've never won one of those fights yet, and you're not going to win this next one either. So shape up; get your act together before it's too late. Go out with some glory, your head held high.

Listen up, old timer. We've known each other quite a spell. We've always been able to talk. People are saying you can't cut the mustard any more. I'm not one to believe that, but you know how people do talk.

And if you can't pull it off, then here's my last piece of advice. Find yourself a good shrink and get your blizzards checked out. A personality change like you're going through is definitely not normal.

Think it over, you old reprobate! You could just end up out in the cold you know.

February, 1987

# Λ Cheap Shot!

Dear Life:

I've got a few things to say to you, you rat.

You and I have been scrapping for more than three-score years now. Up 'til a couple weeks ago, it's been a pretty fair fight. Oh, you've bent my nose a few times. But I always figured I've come out about even. After all, like the old song, you never promised me a rose garden.

But the other day you belted me good, real good. You put me on the canvas for a mandatory eight count. And you did it with a sucker punch, a cheap shot below the belt!

Oh, you set me up beautifully, you jerk. For the last three years you led me down your primrose path; smiling, happy, lulling me to sleep in false complacency. You let me feel the push of cool trout streams against my legs, and you let me toddle grandchildren on my knee. You let me chase a dream of putting words on paper, and you let me feel good inside when people said they liked them.

Oh, you bum, you did a beautiful job! You let me sit out on that little lake snapping fat bluegills and crappies from a hole in the ice until dusky night had settled. And then, when I'd completely dropped my guard, you threw that sucker punch.

And I felt it. It hurt -- but not too bad. At first I thought that twinge of pain, the cramp in my lower back where your fist had landed, was from bending over that hole all afternoon. I wasn't worried.

But when the chills and the hot flashes took turns putting beads of sweat on my forehead as I headed home, I knew I'd been had.

You chuckled as I came in the door, as I told Momma, "I don't feel good!" And you laughed as I came up the basement stairs and called to her, "I'm going to pass out!"

And you roared with sadistic glee as the floor came up to meet me halfway between the dining room and the bedroom. You creep! You scared the bejeebers out of that good woman! My foggy brain could hear it in her voice as she bent over me pleading, "Where does it hurt? Where does it hurt?" You had no right to do that.

And you were really enjoying yourself a half-hour later as I laid writhing and moaning in the hospital emergency room, as I felt the doctor's probing.

"Classic symptoms of a kidney stone," the words came. "If it is, it'll break the Guiness Book of Records," I groaned to Momma. "It's gotta be a BOWLING BALL!"

You'd flattened me, that was easy to see. The tubes, the plastic bottles, the bags hooked to me as I laid in that hospital bed told the full story.

But you overlooked a couple things. You forgot about my handlers, the doctors and nurses that worked on me in that corner of the ring, binding my wounds. And you forgot about the friends that came to sit by my bedside, their cheers; the words they said and wrote. Words they waved under my nose like bottles of smelling salts.

Three days it took me to answer the bell. And just as I staggered out of my corner, you threw your best haymaker - - your "possible blockage" upper cut. And you really put me down with that one.

You sent me reeling off to a specialist, my brain rattled like it's never been addled before. I wasn't ready for that shot. I wasn't prepared for options ranging from infection to -- well, you know the word.

And I told the world exactly what I thought of you. If my good wife had never before had grounds to tell me to stuff it, she had them that day. The nice receptionist, I told her. And the nurse and even the doctor, I gave them all my version of you in no uncertain terms.

Then the good news. Your uppercut hadn't really landed. I'd ducked at the last instant. And I began to come to. My senses came back, back to where the next day I was so ashamed that I called the good doctor to issue a conscience-cleansing apology.

I'm not going to forget this, old buddy. From now on, you're no longer Mr. Nice Guy. I know now that I can't trust you, and I'm going to be as wary as a trap-shy timber wolf. I'm going to watch every move you make.

You'll remember that you and I made a deal three years ago. Ten years, I told you I wanted; years of good health, years I figure I've earned.

So I'm telling you now, keep your mitts off of them. Fight fair and we'll get along just fine.

Sincerely,

Your Old Sparring Partner

March, 1988

# Backyard Bossy

Those of you that read this column may recall an account last fall about Momma and the backyard buck. Now we have a case of Momma and the backyard bossy!

In the instance of the buck, the deer dropped dead in our backyard. With our bossy, it was I that almost dropped dead.

"What the heck is that!" I hollered, astonished as I looked out the kitchen window.

Momma and I had just returned from a vacation trip to Missouri. And as I carried the first load of suitcases into the house, I'd glanced out the back window. There on the edge of our pine tree windbreak stood a cow, a black and white Holstein balefully eyeing the house.

"I can't believe it!" Momma answered as she took a look. Both of us were in "udder" shock. There Bossy stood; unmoving, unblinking, her eyes fixed in a stupefied stare as only cows can stare.

And then it dawned on us. Bossy was a fake, a contented cow capriciously cut from plywood. But done so lifelike that at first glance from its hundred feet distance, both Momma and I had been completely taken in.

And not only us. An hour or so later, I'd gone to get Butch, our dog, from where he'd been boarding while we were away. And as I walked him into the backyard toward his kennel, he took one look at the strange new critter that had invaded his domain.

"Woof!" he barked and planted all four of his feet, the hair on his back standing on end. It took some fair leash pulling and sweet talking to coax him over for a sniff of Bossy.

And then the fun part of the mystery began. Who was responsible for this dastardly deed? Who would have the courage, the cunning to concoct a cockeyed cow? Like right now, Momma's brain began to spin.

Well, she's pretty good at cold tracking cuprits. Like Sherlock Holmes, she set her mind to the case. And as her investigation began, back came the good-natured barbs of rebuttal.

For example. A phone call. The neighbor next door was on the line. "Say," she said, "Isn't there a city ordinance about keeping livestock in the city?" I agreed there was and admitted I might get thrown in jail.

From across the street, another neighbor. "Say," she said, "When are you going to build a barn for that poor cow?" I agreed that one would be needed.

And then the first clue. Momma was discreetly questioning a third neighbor. "I sure wish I knew who put that thing there," she said as the two stood gazing at the bodacious bovine.

The response was first a faint hint of a smile, then a little snicker, and last a deep hearty laugh. "I know," she said, "But I'm sworn to secrecy." Progress! At least we now knew that somebody knew.

And the charade continued. Out came the cameras to record the event for posterity; a polaroid shot to send to the relatives in Missouri to show them what had greeted us on our return.

Next a windy day. Quickly it became obvious that Old

*Marian Becker and her backyard "cow."*

Bossy was totally tipsy, her flat feet not up to supporting her bounteous bod. Out I went, a drill in hand to bolt her to a steel post hammered into the ground with my wood-splitting maul. Such a masterpiece of cow art had to be displayed properly, not flat on its behind in the pine needles.

Then finally, a breakthrough in Momma's sleuthing.

The phone rang. Ann Walker was calling. John, her husband, is one of my fishing pals.

The conversation began innocently. "How are you? Did you have a nice trip? Was the weather nice in Missouri?" All very innocent chit chat -- too innocent.

And Momma sensed that something was fishy. "Do you know, someone put a full-sized cow in our backyard," she told Ann. Silence on the other end, then a muffled, half-choked chuckle.

"I thought it might be you guys!" Momma said. And the confession blurted out.

"John saw one of those cows down in Florida last winter. And he said to me 'Becker's gotta have one of those'! So he rushed right out and made you folks one."

The cow caper case had been solved. "We hope you like it," Ann continued, sounding a bit unsure. "If you don't, we'll take it back."

"No way," I told her. "That cow stays. It goes with the chickens in the kitchen!"

Besides, it's not often that I get to milk a cow for a story.

May, 1989

# Not Dry Behind The Ears!

There's an old saying that goes, "The best things in life are free!"

The little envelope came in the mail recently. I opened it and found a "thank you" note; a simple little note, obviously handmade, handprinted in old style English script lettering. It was signed, "The Terraceview Residents." Terraceview is a nursing home in Shell Lake.

I value the card. I won't be throwing it away.

One of the side benefits of writing this column has been several invitations to speak to people in nursing homes, a half-dozen appearances going back to last winter. I try to give something to brighten their day. And in return I receive.

Take for instance the visit with a group of men patients, an early morning gathering that they periodically hold where they have breakfast together and invite a speaker to join them.

I was there well-ahead of time, and I spent a minute or two going from table to table chatting with the old gentlemen, hopefully giving them a chance to warm up to me. My game plan was to talk to them about the outdoors; fishing, hunting, logging, old-time farming.

Well, the bacon and eggs and pancakes were served, and we handled them in good shape. Finally, the time came for me to stand up and do my thing.

Now, I figured it would be a good idea to introduce myself by giving some information about my background. Things like my family, jobs I've had, how I grew up, hobbies. So I went through my spiel, and at the end I said I was sixty years old. I thought that little fact would establish some rapport, some kinship with my audience.

No sooner were those words out of my mouth when from the back of the room up pipes a voice that says, "You aren't even dry behind the ears yet!"

Life is all relative. And I guess when you're ninety, you have a right to look at someone thirty years your junior as a young whippersnapper. Anyway, it was one of the nicest compliments I've been paid in a long, long time.

I've always felt that I could relate fairly well with older people. Perhaps it's because as a youngster I was close to my grandfathers and grandmothers. I had great grandparents. There are good memories of talking to a grandfather as he smoked his pipe in an old rocking chair next to a wood-fired cook stove; of helping a grandmother gather eggs in her hen house.

So I've received a fair share of satisfaction from my recent visits with those fine elderly people. To be sure it's easier for me to put a presentation together for the menfolks than for the ladies. But I seem to be doing OK. With the ladies I rely more on slide pictures that I've taken. I show them pictures of Momma and the grandkids for instance, tell them little stories about them. Things like that.

But they seem to like the pictures of wildflowers the best. I show them scenes of trilliums, violets, appleblossoms. And I like to hear them say, "Aren't they pretty!" or "I always liked violets." I guess I've learned that no matter how old a lady is, she'll always like flowers.

The menfolks, they like their fishing and hunting.

I'll never forget the touching experience during one of my visits last winter. I'd brought along a muskie rod and reel and an ultralight spinning outfit that I use for trout.

My plan was to pass the rods around the room, to let the men handle the rods. I began my talk, and I handed the muskie rod to a gentleman nearest me, a man in a wheelchair, expecting him to pass it on.

Well, I continued to talk, but the rod never got passed. I paused, and I could see why. The light in his eyes told me, Finally, I was forced to reach for the rod, ask him to give it up, and hand it on.

When I finished my talk, the old gentleman motioned to me to come over to him. He proceeded to tell me that he was ninety-three years old, that he loved to fish. And then he reached into his pocket for his billfold. From it, he took a yellowed clipping from a newspaper, and he held it up for me to see.

It was a picture of a man, a much younger man, holding a twenty-four pound northern pike.

"This is me," he said.

June, 1987

# Test-Tube Tinkering

All this talk going around about genetic engineering is leaving me cold.

Genetic engineering is the new wave of scientific experimentation. Scientists are trying to develop super strains of plants and animals.

The other day I was driving down the road listening to the car radio. Paul Harvey came on. Harvey proceeded to explain how genetic engineering is being used to try to grow fish that will eat pollution.

So what's new. Seems to me we've already got fish like that. Unless I'm reading those PCB and mercury health advisory warnings all wrong.

But I've been into genetic engineering for over twenty years. I wish someone had told me I was. I wish some of those test-tube tinkerers would come and visit me. I'd like to show them some results of my work.

True, I haven't succeeded in producing anything that will benefit mankind right now. But then who knows what the future will bring.

Take my yard for instance. That's where I do all my research. I've produced some weird variations of plants and animals.

For example, I have a strain of robins that defies imagination. Now, robins have a reputation of being among the elite of the bird world. The robin is our state bird. Kids and senior citizens love robins.

Well, I'll tell you my robins are different. Every spring they come back from a winter of loafing in the magnolia trees of the sunny south. Oh, we're happy to see them.

But then the crazy, irrational behavior of my subspecies begins. Each morning at the crack of dawn they start pounding their heads against the bedroom windows. Momma tries pulling the drapes, putting up black plastic bags. Nothing works. All day it's peck, peck, peck!

Then the nest building starts. This year in the yew bush right by the garden hose. Come near the bush and a fiendish, screeching, feathered divebomber buzzes your head, almost taking your hair off.

Our robins aren't nice, sweet, cuddly things. They're weird, and they're mean. But they're survivors, and I'm proud of them. I don't have to worry about robins becoming extinct now that I've perfected a superbird.

Let's talk about my work in the plant world. I've really been successful there. Take my dandelions and my crab grass. They're shining examples.

My neighbor Zino Tully has a lawn you could shoot pool on. Every blade lies exactly where it's suppose to, like the freshly-combed hair of a six-year-old in Sunday school.

But he's got wimpy weeds. My weeds are full-bodied, heavy-muscled jobs. Weeds that look like they're on steroids. Last year I had crab grass so macho that it threatened to eat up the concrete driveway, a classic example of how genetic engineering can get out of hand. One has to be careful when tampering with nature.

And my dandelions. They're vigorous, broad-shouldered specimens that stand tall with handsome yellow blossoms.

Years ago my grandfather always liked a mess of dandelion greens each spring. Laced with dressing of bacon grease and vinegar; he'd say, "They'll put hair on your chest!"

Who knows, someday we may have a food shortage. Should such a crisis arise, my dandelions will be ready and waiting.

Like I said, I got into this genetic engineering thing without knowing it, by accident actually. At the beginning, trying to be a good citizen and neighbor, I fought my weeds. I declared war on weeds. I poked and pulled, dug and sprayed.

But then I suddenly realized that weeds were an important part of our economy. Watch TV. Read the ads. You'll see how much of our gross national product is generated by weeds. Hoes, rakes, shovels, sprayers, gadgets of all kinds.

Get rid of weeds and a lot of people would be out of work. We need good weeds in this country.

In my modest, humble way I'm trying to do my bit. I can't say that I've got the best weeds in the world, but I'm working on it.

This spring my good neighbor gave me some advice. Buy some of that super-duper combination fertilizer-weed killer stuff. Put it on the lawn.

Well, I did. And I got some interesting results. My dandelions looked up at me; their yellow faces smiling like Charlie Cool, my grandson, when you set a dish of ice cream in front of him.

And the crabgrass. One particularly "lush" plant raised its quivering blades and softly whispered, "Make mine a double, will ya' pal!"

June, 1988

# Logging Lore

Logging camps... river drives... narrow gauge rail-roads... all pages in the history of our forests here in northern Wisconsin.

A little magazine came in the mail the other day; my copy of "Chips and Sawdust," a publication put out by the Forest History Association of Wisconsin. The group is comprised of people in the forestry, logging, and timber manufacturing fields; folks who are dedicated to preserving some of our colorful lumbering past, an era that goes back to the virgin timber days at the turn of the century.

It's an effort that I applaud.

For the words that appear each week in this column are written in a mini-forest history atmosphere; here in my basement "wreck" room, which I decided years ago would have an old logging camp decor--- rough-sawn hemlock panelling on the walls and time-worn crosscut saws, cant hooks, peavies, and double-bitted axes hanging there from.

Not that I'm an authority on Wisconsin forest history. But with almost forty years of ramming around in the far corners of our backwoods, I've had fair opportunity to see some of the remains of the early logging days. The traces are there if you have an eye for them, written on the land in old railroad grades, splash dams and camp sites.

But time is slowly taking its toll on the old evidence.

Back in the 1950's, when most of my workdays were spent in the woods cruising and mapping timber, recognizing the old relics was relatively easy. And I came upon many long-abandoned logging campsites. What a thrill it was to poke around in the ruins and ponder how the lumberjacks lived and worked in those places.

And over time, I've had the pleasure of meeting and getting to know some of those old-time lumberjacks. Nels Olson of Mason, for example. In his book, "Time in Many Places," Olson describes in authentic detail, life in the old camps and sawmills where he worked as a young man.

Another lumberjack who turned author was George Corrigan of Saxon who, in his book "Calked Boots and Cant Hooks," tells of the early-century logging days in the Mellen area. Long ago, I once had the privilege of spending a day in the woods with George. And later we corresponded about a second book he was contemplating.

Then a lumberjill, Esther Gibbs, of Spooner. Esther also wrote a book, "We Went A Loggin'." And in it she tells of times after World War I when she and her husband worked as cooks for a large logging camp in the Chippewa River country south of Ladysmith. Her accounts of camp life are some of the most descriptive I've read.

There were others, men who didn't write books, but still could tell the stories. Like Leo Gould, the old forest ranger at Tomahawk, who told me about log drives on the Prairie River into Merrill. How, on the spring mornings, the jacks would be a bit slow getting into the cold water. And how the boss in his thick Irish brogue would yell, "Get in there! It won't bu-r-r-rn ya!"

And some of the old-timers I worked with in the 60's on the Menominee Indian forest east of Antigo! Like Alex

Waupoose. Alex was the logging superintendent, responsible for all the cutting in the woods. He and I worked closely. A wonderful gentlemen, I enjoyed his accounts of the old days.

Then Bogue Dickie, a Menominee logger. I got to know Bogue well in my visits to his jobs. And I cherish the moments we spent together, sitting on big yellow birch logs, visiting. He'd tell about the old camps; of the narrow-gauge railroads that hauled the logs before trucks came to the woods. Of the log drives down the Wolf and Oconto rivers that he took part in, and the dangerous log jams he witnessed.

There's a home-made coffee table here, standing nearby as I write. It's one I made many years ago from an ancient rusty circular saw, a blade that came from an old sawmill. Gordon Fleming, a logger I knew in the 50's over at Park Falls, gave it to me.

The old saw reposes quietly now. Yet, I find myself looking at it and wondering how many big white pine logs it sawed into lumber, how many long-gone woodsmen listened to its whine.

It's a genuine piece of Wisconsin's forest history, a gift from a genuine Wisconsin lumberjack.

June, 1991

# North-Country Woodsman

Over the years, as I've walked the trails of the outdoors, a fair number of unique people have crossed my path. They're folks who stood out from the crowd, individuals who followed different compass readings, guys who drank only from their own canteens.

Such is Sid Hovey. Hovey's half Alaska sourdough, half north-country woodsman, and half fisherman of many points in between, I say!

I know! I know! That adds up to three halves! But that's not unrealistic. For Sid Hovey has seen considerably more of life's sides than the average person.

I met Hovey recently on a visit to the cabin my brother Bill and his wife Sandy have over in the Winchester country of Vilas County, a summer home that's tucked deep in the forest, where the hemlocks and maples stand so thick that their shade is almost night-like at mid-day.

"You have to meet my neighbor, Sid!" Bill had said as Momma and I unpacked. "He lives over there across the lake. He's coming over for supper tomorrow night. When we go out fishing tonight we'll stop at his place and I'll introduce you."

That evening, as we headed out for a try at the walleyes, Bill slipped the boat alongside Hovey's dock. And from a meticulously-maintained cottage that his wife refers to as "Sid's museum," emerged the tall, broad-shouldered Hovey; a man who, at 70, still enjoys slipping a packsack filled with grub onto his back and heading into the woods.

That evening, and the next, I got to know the man, as he allowed me to peek into his life, telling story after story of his experiences. He's retired now, after a long career with the Alaska Highway Commission and the United States Forest Service on the Ottawa National Forest in Upper Michigan.

His life's work was in road design, construction and maintenance, duties that often led him into uncharted territory, like the glacier country of Alaska.

He told of the time forty years ago when he was travelling the Alcan highway, a gravel road that traversed some of the wildest, most remote, terrain in North America. A culvert had washed out, and while attempting to cross the gully, Sid's car got hung up. There he was, miles from nowhere, stuck.

"I looked up the road," he said. "There stood two animals. I thought they were moose. But they were a team of horses driven by a woman. And when she got to me, we hooked onto my Ford and out it came. She didn't want anything, but I insisted she take ten dollars."

And a time in Alaska when he was driving a lonely back road. Up ahead, from out of the bush, stepped a man with a packsack on his shoulders. Hovey stopped to give him a lift. The man was a prospector, it turned out, and the two got into a discussion about gold. Which the old prospector summarized by saying, "You know, there's plenty of gold in this country. But there's an ENORMOUS amount of gravel mixed with it!"

At one time Hovey himself got the gold fever. "I gave up everything else," he said, "all my fishing. I even had my own sluiceway."

And our conversation shifted to fishing. How in his Alaska

*Sid Hovey learned to appreciate Eskimo artwork during his years in Alaska.*

years he paddled canoes up lonely rivers to catch cutthroat trout, while big brown bears prowled the banks. Trout fishing remains today dear to his heart, and he regularly fishes wild upper peninsula streams like the Huron, Montreal, and the Two Hearted River for steelhead rainbows, drifting home-made yarn flies through the fast runs.

He takes trips far out on Lake Superior to jig for lake trout in the summer and whitefish through the ice in winter. And he likes his muskies, as the 29-pounder that hangs from the wall of his cabin, a fish he caught last fall, shows.

While in Alaska, he developed a strong interest in the art-work of the native Indian and Eskimo people. Miniature repli-cas of some of that art, wooden faces and totem poles that he's carved and painted, adorn his cabin.

"Totem poles represent family trees of clans," he said, "not religious meaning. Some are 40 feet tall in Alaska. But mak-ing them is becoming a lost art."

Nearby in a storage shed, rest three prized watercraft, two canoes and a 14-foot boat, all hand-fashioned of cedar and spruce. One canoe, an 18-footer made in New Brunswick, Canada, is so stable that Hovey uses it on Lake Superior. The boat, an Old Town Maine model, is at least 60 years old.

Through all our discussion, hung a deep insight and philos-ophy about life and its values, the good and the not-so-good.

Life, after all, is a lot like the gold the old prospector spoke of. For sure, there's a lot of gold to be found in life. But there's also an ENORMOUS amount of gravel mixed with it.

...The trick, of course, is to separate the two.

August, 1995

# Travelling By Snowshoe

I strapped on the snowshoes the other day and took a hike back into the tree farm.

Years ago I spent a lot of time on showshoes. People like loggers, timber cruisers, wildlife managers that work out-doors in northern Wisconsin get very familiar with snow-shoes. True, the snowmobile and the ATV have taken some of the strain out of this ancient form of travel. But there comes a point where one has to get off the machine and walk.

In a bad winter when the snow comes early and deep, snowshoeing can be rough duty. The shoes are supposed to support the wearer and allow a person to float rather easily. But when the white stuff is soft and fluffy, one sinks deep; and a good pair of legs is needed to take a steady diet of woods work.

Mid-March was always the best time for snowshoeing. With the warm sun and the cold nights, the snow settles and a crust forms. Then if you got going early in the morning, a lot of ground could be covered. One could almost enjoy snowshoeing.

Snowshoes go back a long time. I've read accounts of Indian people fashioning shoes from saplings and deer hide.

My first experience with snowshoes was in the early 50's. The shoes back then were pretty good, the frames made of strips of bent white ash and the webbing of rawhide. Those old shoes however, required considerable care. Periodically they'd have to be varnished to keep the wood and rawhide waterproof. Shoes that soaked up water got heavy and wore out quickly. A smart woodsman wouldn't let that happen.

Today's shoes are still made with ash frames, but neoprene has replaced rawhide for webbing. Neoprene is both tough and waterproof, a big improvement over the old days.

Three styles of snowshoes are commonly seen here in Wisconsin; the "trail" model, the "bearpaw" and the "Michigan."

The trail model is a long narrow shoe built for open, fairly straight-line travel where a minimum of turning is done. The bearpaw on the other hand, is a short oval-shaped shoe designed for thick, brushy going. Bearpaws are frequently worn by trappers who get into swampy cover along streams a lot.

The Michigan shoe is a compromise between the other two. Tear-shaped, wide at the toe and narrow at the heel, it's best for average woods conditions.

Shoes come in different sizes. The bigger the individual, the bigger the shoe needed for support. Woodsmen talk about "fourteen forty-eights" and "fifteen fifty-twos." What they mean is that the shoe is fourteen inches wide and forty-eight inches long, for example.

But the most important part of a snowshoe is the sandal, the little harness in which the wearer's boot is placed. Most commonly made from leather, I've seen many models over the years. A smart individual years back invented a sandal made from old truck innertubes, and it worked well.

The sandals I use now are again made from neoprene. They're excellent because they're tough, waterproof and don't stretch; assuring a nice, tight, constant fit.

And the proper mounting of the sandal on the shoe is critical. When the wearer's boot is strapped into the sandal, the tip of the boot should just clear the cross-piece of the frame of the snowshoe. There's nothing more uncomfortable than trying to walk with the toe of your boot rubbing the cross-piece. Properly mounted, the weight of the snowshoe should ride from the ball of the foot. Walking then will be a smooth, fluid, natural motion.

The most memorable snowshoe trip I ever made was with an old-time timber cruiser some thirty-five years ago. A strong-minded individual, he was a highly-respected woodsman. For a young rookie to be asked to help him was an honor.

Well, one day my old friend asked me to give him a hand to examine some timber. We'd have to snowshoe three miles down an unplowed firelane just to get near the land. Neither of us relished the thought.

The plan was to snowshoe in the first day. Break a trail, we called it. Then come back the second to do the work. So we did, taking turns leading with the hard work of breaking the trail. And when we got to the end of the three miles, there we found the lane freshly-plowed from the other direction

Let's just say that my outspoken old friend spoke out with some very clear and distinct language.

March, 1988

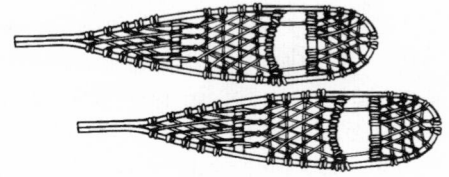

# Kicking Tires

Well, I've been out kicking tires again!

What I'm saying is this, I traded my pickup; something I do every three years or so. And once again, I'm proud to say, I've survived that grand old American tradition. Not without considerable agony and anguish, however.

My "Triennial Truck-Trading Trauma," I call the ritual!

It's an experience, believe me! But then, I need not point that out. You folks trade trucks and cars too.

With me, the awesome affair begins in late summer, when I read the ads in the papers and see the commercials on TV, that the model year is coming to a close. And big "clearance sales" are on. Maybe I'll get something in the mail, like a little reminder that I'm eligible for a tempting morsel called a "rebate."

It's then, each morning, as I climb into the old buggy, that I find myself eyeing more critically the mileage on the speedometer. And, following that, I find myself mentally assessing the condition of my checkbook. The two go hand-in-hand, as you well know.

"Hmmmm!" I think to myself. "Well, it won't hurt to look around a bit. After all, I don't HAVE to trade!"

And just to make sure I've got my backside covered, I find an appropriate moment to let Momma in on my thinking; casually, when she's nice and relaxed, like after supper as she's watching the Cubs.

"You know," I'll say, "it might be a good time to shop around for a new pickup."

Well, this year, let me tell you, she set me straight on where she stood on new pickups.

"OK," she said. "But don't come home with one unless it's got air conditioning! And automatic transmission too! You keep saying you want me to help out with the driving on our trips."

"But those things cost more money," I came back.

"I don't care," she answered. "We're only old once, you know!"

Air and automatic, I dutifully note in my memory.

And off to the dealers, I go... to do my tire-kicking. There's the usual round of salutations and how's-fishing questions. But then, the party begins to get rough, real rough.

Sticker prices! One look at the prices on the new jobs, and I find myself gasping for breath, like I'm going into terminal cardiac arrest.

But all is not gloom and doom, the salesmen explain. There's an array of rebates, for which I may qualify; depending on which "package" I select, of course.

And so the serious arm wrestling begins. Personally, I like salesmen with private offices, places where we can go at it hammer-and-tong without the whole world listening in. And I like salesmen wearing white shirts, and never sunglasses! I like to see my salesmens' eyes when I'm doing my serious arm wrestling!

Well, to make a long story short, after three or four weeks of heavy hammer-and-tong-type negotiation, I finally cut a deal. I'd started out looking for a plain-Jane type truck. But instead, I ended up with one that's loaded with doodads; the result of a package deal in which, as was explained, I got all those trinkets free. Hah!

And in due time, I removed the collection of outdoor junk from my old buggy, said goodbye to that faithful friend, and moved into my new blue home-away-from-home.

The other day, as I was heading out for an afternoon of muskie fishing with Charlie Tollander down on Bone Lake, some thoughts crossed my mind.

Outside the white-wall tires spun on the highway. Inside, in the cab, from the tape deck came the music of George Jones and Tammy Wynette, as the cruise control rolled me effortlessly down the road.

And from the dim recesses of my brain came a picture from the past... that of a dirt-poor country boy in baggy bib overalls, a slingshot hanging from his back pocket, walking barefoot along a dusty road, whistling to himself.

Old Plain-and-Simple may never be the same.

That's for sure.

September, 1991

# Pursuing The Rummage Sale Dream

Well folks, it's time for my annual report to you on my good wife's rummage sale activities for the year.

Last year, you may recall, I covered the emotional side of rummage saleing. The thrill of bagging an eight-point potato masher in the far corner of a garage as the sun peeks pink over the eastern horizon. The joy of nine old rolling pins standing tall in the corner of the kitchen. The tear that curls gently down her cheek at the sight of an ancient eggbeater, rescued as it was about to be dispatched to an unmarked grave in the town dump.

This year I will report to you on more serious things... the hard work, the personal sacrifice, the economics that go with pursuing the rummage sale dream.

But first, let me say that Momma has had another good year. She bagged some fine trophies.

Three more rolling pins have been added to her collection. And one is a real prize, perhaps so rare that it may be the only one of its kind. I'd dare say that it ranks right up there with a Rembrandt painting or a Stradivarius violin. It's a rolling pin with class.

I say that because on the foot-long roller, hand-printed in classic style in well-worn ink, are a half-dozen recipes for goodies like cookies and pie crusts.

How ingenious! What could be more innovative than to

have your favorite recipe flashing before your eyes as you roll out the dough for a batch of oatmeals or a lemon pie! Words like "one cup of sugar" and "three cups of flour." Oh, if that old rolling pin could talk, what a story it would tell.

But I'm digressing. Let me get back to the down-to-earth, behind-the-scenes action that goes on in the rummage sale business. Being successful isn't easy. Like the well-trained athlete who excels on the field, there's hard work and sacrifice that goes into preparing for the weekly Friday morning game.

Take the travel for instance. Momma puts in a fair amount of time on the road. Any salesman will tell you that's no fun. Let me illustrate my point.

My hunting and fishing jaunts have taken me into the far corners of the hinterlands. I figure I know the back roads pretty good.

Well, not any more. She knows the country better than I do.

We were up to Hayward one night this summer. On the way home I decided to cut across on a county road. Well, I ran into a detour. So I backed into a little brushy trail to turn around, a road I'd hesitate to take the pickup down.

"What are you turning around for?" she asked, giving me her patented disgust look. "That road goes through."

And then there's the economic side of rummage sales. You have to know your stuff in an active marketplace -- let me elaborate.

Forty years ago back in college I took an economics course, Econ 101. I cut a big fat "C" in that course. So what if I had to stay up all night before the final exam and memorize the textbook. I passed the course, and I figured that qualified me as an "expert" in economics -- simple things like the federal reserve system, international banking, and the gold standard for the dollar! I don't recall rummage sales being mentioned, however.

Well, last year I was helping Momma get ready for her very own yearly sale. It would be one of those "catch and release" deals where she gathers a pile of treasures and then recycles them back into the environment for everyone to enjoy once more.

*Two young rummage sale customers are served by Marian Becker.*

As I worked in the garage, I happened to pick up one of those little wicker baskets that you line with a fancy cloth napkin and serve hot biscuits in when company comes over. There on the handle was Momma's little masking tape price tag -- twenty-five cents.

But there on the bottom was the old price tag -- fifty cents.

"How can you make money buying something for fifty cents and selling it for a quarter?" I innocently asked.

She gave me another of her patented disgust looks.

"You sure don't know anything about the economics of rummage sales. I've had twenty-five cents worth of fun out of that basket. Money isn't everything you know!" she informed me.

My old professor didn't cover that point back in Econ 101. Obviously he wasn't a rummage saler.

September, 1987

# Warm Wind

A warm wind blew across the land the other day. And riding its wings, was that mischievous imp of a maid, Miz Spring, vivaciously blowing kisses across the landscape.

Like a knight riding a white charger she came, sweeping the snowbanks from the fields and sending those remaining fleeing in retreat for last ditch stands to woods and forests.

On the north side of the driveway, she cut through the last of the crusted ridge of dirty ice and snow, exposing for the first time since December the brown lawn beneath. The melt water and the sunshine mixed to send forth a first faint blush of green from the dormant grass.

And I rejoiced.

I watched as the warm wind ruffled the feathers of the chickadees perched on the bird feeder outside the dining room window. They paused, as if contemplating some primeval instinct, then flitted in joyful, bouncing flight into the nearby woods, to search out their natural foods, seeds and bugs and insect larvae. Happy it seemed, to at last be free of their dependence on man's sunflower seeds and beef suet.

The view in the backyard is not pretty to some. "Yuck!" Momma says, as she ponders the remnants of cruddy recalcitrant snowbanks and the pool of water on the path to the dog kennel, held by the frost-impervious soil.

But I see differently. "The re-birth of life. That's what you see out there," I tell her. And while I see a ton of work to be tackled shortly, like chips and bark from the remains of the woodpile and leaves to be raked; I can also see the miracle of creation taking place, as sunshine and moisture and soil begin to work their mysterious magical chemistry.

As the warm wind swept across the land, the melting snow sent trickles of water down hillsides into valleys where they joined, forming rivulets. Some flowed noisily onward, feeding into streams where trout stirred at the influx of their warmth.

Others moved slowly, almost imperceptibly, into marshes and swamps, wetlands where the precious moisture would be stored, recharging the groundwater... Mother Nature's bank account to be drawn upon when the droughts of July and August burn hot against the land.

The soft breaths of Miz Spring wafted gently through Rollie Schaefer's sugar bush. There, the tall maples caught the breeze, swaying gently before it. And in their upper branches, thousands of pale yellow buds began to respond, swelling, calling for the nutrients stored far below in the trees' roots, still encased by frost. And upward, along the trunks, through the tubelike vessels of the cambium just under the bark, the maple sap began to flow.

Rollie was ready, waiting. With his power drill, he augured holes in the maples, inserted spiles, and hung his pails to intercept the sweet liquid. And in due time, Oscar Johnson will fuel the fires of the evaporator he tends each spring up the road, to change the sap into amber syrup, topping for pancakes, waffles, and ice cream sundaes.

The warm wind caught the eye of farmers across the countryside, sending manure spreaders clattering over frost-firm fields in early mornings after the milking was done. In machine sheds equipment will be gone over, loose bolts tightened the grease fittings filled. And in evenings, after supper, calculations made of fertilizer and seed oats orders.

Too, one of Miz Spring's smooches caressed my own cheek, reviving a spirit that had laid dormant within me. The thrill recalled my old country school days, when the end of winter also meant the end of bulky sheepskin mackinaws and heavy four-buckle overshoes. Feet seemed to take wings, and recesses were filled with marble shooting and softball playing, rites of spring passage.

...To the tree farm I was drawn. And there in one of my spruce plantations, that will-of-the-wisp, Miz Spring, and I embraced.

There, as my booted feet sloshed in the half-snow, half-water standing in the furrows, I trimmed the twigs of soon-to-be Christmas trees. The piney clean smell of spruce pitch caught my nostrils. I watched as glistening beads formed on the severed branch tips. In the nearby oaks, the music of a woodpecker tapping out a tune came to my ears. And I listened.

Miz Spring was passing by. Lordy, but that lady's beautiful!

April, 1991

# Holiday Maladies

Well, I think Momma and I are going to make it. We were down over the holidays, down with the PHIT and the PHEW.

What are the PHIT and the PHEW? They're bad news. PHIT is "pre-holiday induced trauma." And PHEW is "post-holiday emotional wipeout." Some scientists believe they're really one ailment, just two stages. I tend to agree with that theory.

Momma usually catches a worse case of the PHIT than I do. But I get the PHEW worse than she does. Anyway, we're feeling better, starting to get back on our feet.

PHIT often hits about halfway between Thanksgiving and Christmas. You know when you've got it when you're tired all the time, start getting irritable, and tempers get touchy. Get it bad and one goes through what's known as "phitting out."

PHIT's cause is not completely known. But there's strong evidence (based on my own research) that it's caused by something called "getting ready for Christmas."

Christmas shopping, for example, can trigger a severe attack of PHIT with Momma. Christmas shopping means decisions; what to buy, for whom, how much to spend. Compounding the whole thing is the fact that the decisions have to be made in secrecy. That makes her more susceptible to PHIT.

Oh, she tries hard to avoid the malady. For instance, she does some of her shopping out of catalogs. Now that sounds simple, easy. Not true. One night she was poring over her reference library; scowling, fussing. And when she finally gave up and went to get her jammies on, I walked over to see what was going on.

Well, I tell you I never saw such a heap of Sears and Penneys and Miles Kimballs. I counted them just for the heck of it. Twenty-eight! Twenty-eight catalogs. No wonder she catches the PHIT!

I wish she'd listen to me, watch me shop. Every year I reserve two hours for my Christmas shopping whether I need it or not. One has to protect one's health.

Back to her gift decisions. The grandchildren are the toughest.

One night she says to me, as she sat agonizing over what to order, "I don't know whether to get one of those new Widgets or a Framdoodle."

"What's the difference?" I ask.

"You'd think you'd know!" she answers, a bit of hostility in her tone.

"Well, tell me!"

"They're cassette players. But the Widget has electronic ignition and the Framdoodle has self-tripping circuit breakers."

The kid's only two.

"So?"

"Well, I think he could use the Widget right now. And we could give him the Framdoodle for his birthday."

"Sounds good to me."

"Besides the Widget plays a cute little song about potty training. To the tune of London Bridges Falling Down."

"Good, the kid could use some of that. London britches

falling down. That is cute."

"Bridges, you dummy! Bridges!" she screams and aims a Sears sale catalog at me.

Heaven knows I try.

Then there's the Christmas cookie baking. A few years ago I wrote a tale about a grandma that gets carried away baking cookies, fills her house up with 'em. Well, the story was pure fiction, of course. But I always wondered what motivated me to write it. Now I know. This year we had to store cookies in the garage.

Next comes the whirl of socializing. Start with the family Christmas Eve get-together; with wrapping paper flying as Charlie Cool opens his Widget package and Butch, our pooch, in the plate of Christmas cookies. It's wild.

I stayed up 'til midnight! Imagine! That's something when you're used to hitting the hay when the street lights come on.

And the next morning, I could feel the PHEW.

"I think I'm catching the PHEW," I said to Momma.

"Get some rest," she says. "We've got two parties this week.

"Two parties in a week!" I groaned. "What are you trying to do, kill me?"

Come New Year's Eve, Momma invites some friends over. She bakes up a big northern I'd caught, stuffs it with wild rice, makes a batch of those fancy potatoes with melted orange cheese on top. And we dig in.

Well, by ten o'clock the PHEW really hit me. There I sat on the sofa, my eyes drooping, my head nodding. Some of the others showed symptoms too.

But Momma comes to the rescue. Over to the kitchen clock she goes, turns the hands two hours ahead, and hands out her paper party hats, her noise makers. And we hoot and holler, kiss and shake hands. After all, it was midnight -- Nova Scotia time.

"Whew, Momma!" I said after the gang had gone. "This PHEW is really rough!"

"Take two aspirins and go to bed," she answers.

I did. By Thanksgiving I should be well.

January, 1989

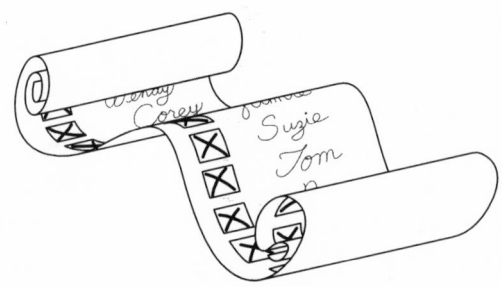

# Painting's Rewards

The backyard scene from Margaret Patchin's picture window was spectacular... sunshine, green grass, golden-hued leaves on the maples and oaks. And the flowers, cascading in color... yellow marigolds, scarlet salvias, and burgundy roses blooming in their fall splendor.

The scene had the appearance of being straight from a master painter's palette. Just like the oil paintings hanging on the walls around me; portraits of the outdoors, of landscapes and seascapes, of trees and mountains and lighthouses.

And that was why I was there, sitting in the Patchin den, visiting with Margaret, to learn about her painting career and the beautiful creations that surrounded us.

"I've done almost a hundred," she told me. "I've given away a lot and sold quite a few."

Not bad for a 76-year-old mother, grandmother, and great-grandmother. Not bad for a lady who's had both hip joints replaced, a knee joint twice, and fights an ongoing battle with asthma, an affliction that requires constant medication and severely limits her activities.

Still, those ailments were a big reason for her getting started with her painting, she explained. "The family had given me some supplies for Christmas one year, paints, brushes, canvases. At the time I said, 'What for! I can't even draw!' "

*Margaret Patchin became a painter as a senior citizen.*

"But then my hips went to pot. I'd always been active, golfing, skiing and gardening. And I couldn't do those things any more."

"We were in Texas at the time, eleven years ago. I just decided I was going to do it. And I told Nancy, my daughter, to send the stuff. Augie Sorenson brought it down."

The Patchins spend their winters at Alamo, Texas, just a few miles from the Mexican border. There Margaret does much of her work.

"I joined the Upper Valley Art League at McAllen," she said. "There's a lot of good artists, mostly senior citizens. I learned a lot by watching other people. That's the only formal training I've ever received."

But as her asthmatic condition has worsened, no longer does she attend the Art League sessions. "The odors from the paints and the turpentine bother me," she said. "So I work at home where I have plenty of ventilation. Last winter I did only two paintings. But this year I hope to do more."

Margaret works strictly in oils on canvas, never on canvasboard. A painting on canvas will hold up for many years without deteriorating, she says.

"I do a lot of blending," she noted. "You don't just paint a sky for example, one color. If you hold that snow to the light," she said, pointing to a winter scene on the wall, "You can see five different colors in it. Mountains and trees are my favorites. I've always been able to do those."

"In their early attempts, artists often make colors too vivid," she continued. "If you're born with a sense of color, you're lucky."

"After you start to paint, you notice every time the sky changes, the lines and the colors. Sometimes people say they've never seen a cloud the color I've painted it. But I don't care... I have."

Patchin's works originate mainly from pictures in artists' books. "But I improvise a lot, incorporating things. I'll often put in something extra," she said.

And the psychic rewards, what are they I asked?

"I like to do things with my hands," she answered. "When I see the finished product, I'm pretty proud."

And Fred, her husband?

"He thinks I'm too much of a perfectionist, but he thinks they're all great. He's given me a lot of encouragement. And he never complains about buying my equipment. Everything's gone up so much. He says, 'So what! It gives you something to do!' "

And that something to do has become something special, a source of pride and self-esteem for a lady who in her own words, "didn't know I had the talent to paint until I forced myself to start."

There's a bit of a lesson there for all of us.

October, 1992

# Yessirree, Bub!

One of the modern miracles of our present-day civilization, I say, is the ball point pen.

I got to thinking about pens the other day. There I sat, suffering from a mild case of writer's block, my trusty pen poised between my forefinger and thumb. Move it sideways, up or down, and squiggly scribblings appeared, like magic, on my yellow notebook paper.

Now there's a neat invention, I thought. And I got to thinking about changes I've seen over the past sixty-something years. There's been a ton of good inventions, I decided. And I went to meditating about some of the best, the top of the line, so to speak!

The thermostat, I decided was the best. The kind that fastens to the wall in my house, and bosses my furnace around. Yessirree, bub! I gave that first place. Having lived through the times of wood burners in the living room, coal furnaces in the basement, and sleeping in longjohns under a feather tick in a frigid, unheated upstairs bedroom, I have no trouble voting for the thermostat as the greatest invention of my time!

Let that baby kick the furnace on in the middle of a January night, and I say to myself, "Ah! This is living!", as I snuggle deeper under the covers.

Automatic chokes on cars came in second. I know, you

younger-generation types out there don't realize there was such a thing as a manual choke.

Well, there was. Back before your time, every Ford and Chevie had a little silver knob on the dash board that said "CHOKE." Nowadays, all the driver has to do is hit the ignition. Bingo! The automatic choke obeys its little computer chip, and the engine purrs.

Not in the old days. Nosirree, bub! You had to have a feather touch on that choke button. "Pull the choke out!" men would holler, not too kindly sometimes, as they twisted the crank on the old buggy. Inside, behind the wheel, the wife would sit, dutifully following instructions. The engine would cough, sputter once or twice, then quit.

"Aw! You flooded it!" the cranker would yell. And doomsday would appear near for us kids. Yessirree, bub! The guy that invented the automatic choke has to go down in history right alongside Thomas Edison and the Wright brothers.

Stainless steel thermos bottles placed third on my list. You don't agree? You say automatic dishwashers, cordless phones, and coffee makers rank higher? No way! The joy that the unbreakable steel thermos bottle has brought to this world can never be measured!

For years, I rattled a lunch box on my way to work in the morning. In it, was always one of those pint glass-lined thermoses. Stand that baby up after pouring a cup of coffee, accidently give it a little bump; and crash, all you had inside was a zillion pieces of broken glass. Another thermos down the tube!

Not so with these modern stainless jobs. Nosirree, bub! You can hammer on those babies and they'll keep your coffee hot. Toss that hummer in the boat, bounce it on the floor of the pickup, and there's not one bit of never mind!

Which brings me around to pens. I gave ballpoint pens only an honorable mention... but a very high one. We've got three drawers of ballpoints around our house. All different sizes, shapes and colors. Some with advertising, like from down at the feed mill, some without.

Pens and I go back a long way. Not quite to the goose feather quill that we see the signers of the Declaration of Independence using. But close.

Take my old country school days, for instance. Where Miss Ridge made us practice our penmanship. And with pen and ink yet! Little brown wooden pens that you slipped penny-apiece silver pen points into. Yessirree, bub! Dip that beauty into the ink well in the upper corner of your desk, and scratch away! Thick lines when the ink flowed, skinny lines when it didn't.

And my high school days. That's when "fountain" pens came along. Dastardly beasts with a little lever on the side. Inside was a little rubber sack that filled with ink when you pumped the lever.

Yessirree, bub! Fill that rotten writer, and have ink leak out all over your shirt pocket. And don't forget to carry a bottle of ink along. And a blotter!

That's why I say the ball point pen is a miracle. It changed my life. Along with thermostats, automatic chokes and stainless steel thermos bottles.

Yessirree, bub! They sure did!

November, 1993

# Charlie Cool

Well, Charlie Cool came home from Colorado the other day. He's been out there all winter. He's my newest grandchild, and he's nine months old. His real name is Kyle, but I call him Charlie Cool.

I hadn't seen him since Christmas. He was just a baby then; a giggling, drooling little squirt that kicked and wiggled when his diapers were changed. We got along just fine. I could bounce him on my knee and coax a smile out of him just about any time; except of course when his appetite was up, and he had a bottle on his mind.

But he's changed. I could hear it in the telephone descriptions from his mom and dad. And I could see it in the snapshots that came in the mail that Momma hung on the refrigerator door with those cute and clever little magnets that she finds somewhere. There was a look on his face that told me Young Charlie was becoming Old Charlie.

There was a reason, of course. He's been around! He's been running around Colorado on weekends looking out car windows from his backseat car seat; looking over snow-capped mountains, steep canyons and tall pine forests. He's gazed in wonder at rushing whitewater trout streams, listened to the roar of their rapids. He's helped count herds of elk, mule deer and antelope that moved down from the high country into the basins to spend the winter.

And he's been traipsin' along mountain paths on his dad's
shoulders in one of those backpack baby buggies to study
ancient Hopi Indian cliff dwellings, to ponder old paintings
on the rock faces. He's had a look at history made before our
forefathers came to America's shores, history that I've never
seen.

Then there's his travelling. Travel broadens one they say.
He's been flitting around the friendly skies in big 737 jet lin-
ers. A young man's head is bound to be turned when you get
preferential boarding privileges; when the pretty stewardesses make a big fuss over you, make sure you're comfortable,
warm your bottles, and Ooh and Aah over your mop of
bright red hair.

How's a guy supposed to keep his head on straight? How
are you going to keep him down on the farm after he's seen
the bright lights of places like Minneapolis, Denver, Boston
and Bangor?

You see, he's been out to Maine too, out to visit his other
grandma. Of course, he was the center of attention, the star
of the show. He even had relatives up from New York City
to pay him homage. I've never had anybody from New York
City come to see me. I don't even know anyone in New York
City.

Then take the tooling cross-country on the interstate high-
ways. From his backseat perch he's surveyed the corn fields
of Minnesota and Iowa; the wheat fields of Kansas and
Nebraska; America's bread basket. He's seen the blue waters
of the St. Croix, the Mississippi, the Missouri; waters rich in
heritage.

And he's stayed in fancy motels where special cribs are
made up for him, where he's given the red carpet VIP treatment. He's dined in fancy rooms where the waitresses bring

out special high chairs for him, where he's sucked his formula to soft music and dim lights. And all the while the pretty waitresses Ooh and Aah over that mop of red hair, caress it gently with their fingers. No wonder he's changed. I'd change too if I was treated that way.

I took him on my knee the other day, gave him one of my famous horsey rides, chucked him under the chin. He studied me for a second or two; then gave me his suave, reserved, number one man-of-the-world look. "Hey, Gramps! Cut the kitchy-koo stuff. I'm no kid any more," he seemed to be telling me.

What's a poor grandfather to do? It's a terrible feeling to have a generation gap with your grandson before he's able to talk.

But I've got some advice for you, Charlie. Just don't get too big for your Pampers. You still don't know anything about fishing.

May, 1987

# Steam Engines . . . Romantic Relics!

"Woo-o-o-o! Woo-woo!" the shrill ear-catching whistle rings across the quiet Washburn County, Wisconsin countryside. Then the notes of "O' Susanna."

Bob Romportl of rural Spooner has his steam engine fired up again. And all the neighbors know it.

Romportl, a young man gifted with rare mechanical ability, owns two steam engines.

"I got interested in them a few years back. I heard about a steam engine for sale at an auction at Haugen and went to the sale. The engine was the first I'd ever seen and I dreamed of owning one. It was kinda overpowering," he explained. "The dream came true in July of 1987 when I bought not one but two."

Steam engines are romantic relics of our past. The engines are the dinosaurs of America's industrial revolution. Invented and built in the late 1800's and early 1900's, they represent an era when energy supplies were long but technology was short, a sharp contrast from today.

The ancient steel and brass beasts of burden were the forerunner of the gasoline-powered internal combustion engines we know today.

Steam power served a multitude of purposes in its day; powering ships, trains, steam shovels used in earth-moving, road-building machinery, logging equipment and sawmills.

But nowhere was their impact greater than in the evolution of farming and agriculture.

Steam engines pulled the plows that broke the grassland prairies of the Plains states, creating vast expanses of wheat. And when the crops were ready for harvest, steam engines turned the threshers that extracted the grain.

Romportl's two engines are a New Huber and a New Giant. The Huber is in operating condition, restored by him. The New Giant is partially restored.

"I'm getting close," Romportl said referring to his New Giant. "It's one of only a handful still in existence. Not too many were made." The engine was built in 1903 by the Northwest Thresher Company of Stillwater, Minnesota.

The unit is believed to have worked in the Blue Hills east of Rice Lake and the north shore of Minnesota where it ran a shingle mill. It weighs about 20,000 pounds when loaded with water.

Romportl's New Huber machine was made in 1914 by the Huber Manufacturing Company of Marion, Ohio. Its serial number is 10308. Only about 11,500 were made.

"It came from the Eau Claire Lakes area and was used for stationary power. The engine is in excellent condition. The gears show little wear," he explained.

"I spent a couple months restoring the engine in my shop. I replaced all the missing parts and re-painted everything to its original colors, right down to the pin striping.

"It's almost a disappointment when they're done," he said.

The Huber weighs 28,000 pounds when loaded. It's rated at 25 horsepower which he explained is equal to about a 100 horsepower diesel engine today.

Romportl displays his Huber at antique engine shows and

in parades. The engine is equipped with rubber pads on its wheels for travel. Each engine is required to be tested by state boiler inspectors before it can be run in public.

"They can't be run without certification papers. Wisconsin is a strict state!" he stated. The Huber's boiler is rated for 150 pounds of steam pressure.

Safety is the reason for the controls.

"It takes temperatures of 300 to 350 degrees fahrenheit to boil water under normal operating pressure. In an explosion the water will turn to steam. They'll take off like a rocket, just like a jet. I've heard stories of them flying right over the barn!" he commented.

Safety features are built into the engines. A water glass gauge shows the water level in the boiler, and Romportl watches it closely. "It's critical!" he noted. There's also a relief valve.

And then there's a lead plug in the crown sheet of the boiler. The plug is designed to melt if the water level in the boiler drops too low. Steam is then released which will extinguish the fire.

"Sometimes you'll find an engine where someone has replaced the lead with an iron plug. This is really dangerous," Romportl explained.

Steam engines were designed to burn wood, coal or straw. Straw was the common fuel used in the treeless prairie states.

"You have to have a heck of a hot fire. You had to have a continuous flow of straw," he said. Romportl uses waste slab wood from his sawmill to fire his Huber. "I use a lot," he noted.

The engines are simple in design. A fire box is constructed inside of the boiler. As the fire heats the water in the boil-

*Steam fills the air as Bob Romportl plays a tune on the calliope of his steam engine.*

er, steam is created. The steam is released into a cylinder which drives the piston to produce power. A centrifugal force governor controls the steam feed.

"They're amazing," Romportl stated.

About two hours are needed to build steam pressure from cold water. His Huber engine can use as much as 800 gallons of water in a full day's work. Water tanks are mounted both in front and at the rear. One pint of water boiled away will make 200 gallons of steam.

"I make over a million gallons of steam in a day's operation," he said.

Steam engines were made with three types of boilers. The most common is the "direct flue" model where the fire box is in the rear and the smoke flue in the front.

A second variety is the "return flue" boiler. The fire is built inside the boiler, and the heat and smoke are sent to the front and then returned back to the smokestack in the rear. Romportl's two machines are of this make.

The most rare engine is the "upright flue" model.

Romportl's Huber engine travels at about 2 1/2 miles per hour. A clutch controls the power to the rear wheels. Steering is provided by chain drives to the front wheels. To move the unit backwards, the engine is run in reverse.

"Some engines had power steering and even four-wheel drive back in those old days. You gotta give those oldtime builders credit," he laughed.

A colorful and essential part of the steam engine era was the water wagon or "tender." The cumbersome engines could not easily move to a water source. Made of steel or wood planks, the tenders hauled water to the engines.

Then there was the whistle code used to signal messages. Toots of varying lengths told when water was needed, called neighbors together for the day's work, or sent the alarm when there was a fire.

Romportl has added a calliope to his Huber. "I put an ad in the paper for old steam whistles and was surprised by the response. I picked up enough so I have ten notes, plus one triple tone on the engine itself. I made the calliope myself," he said with pride.

At first he had some problems with steam condensation. But some minor modifications resolved these. The individual whistles can be adjusted to the pitch of the regular musical scale. Bigger whistles are the low notes, the smaller are the high notes.

"I'm still off on a couple notes," he laughed.

Romportl has always been mechanically interested in machines. He considers the steam engine the ultimate antique of machines.

"That's what got this country going. The steam engine was built to last a hundred years. All you needed was wood and water."

"But the majority of them went for scrap in World Wars I and II when steel was needed so badly. Most companies went out of production in the early 1920's."

Rare people like Romportl that possess the interest and talent to preserve the old engines are responsible for maintaining this nostalgic link to our past. By and large, these people are collectors, buffs with a fond affection for the old intriguing inventions.

Romportl is typical.

"They run so quiet. Like they're alive. They've got personality," he told me.

"And most of all, I love that whistle!"

June, 1988

# On The Road To Real America

We hit the four-lane interstate, and I set the cruise control at 65. Momma's buggy stretched out. The car, used to slow-paced rummage sale and grocery store runs, leaped forward... ecstatic, like Butch, my hunting dog, when I unsnap his leash in an Iowa pheasant field.

"Move over Charles Kuralt! Slide aside Willie Nelson! Momma and I are on the road again," I thought -- on our way south, to Missouri for a visit with relatives. But also, looking forward to meeting up with that elusive will-of-the-wisp, Miz Spring.

- - - - - -

Now, I'm not a lover of interstates. I don't enjoy 18-wheelers tailgating me or hot sportscars zipping in and out like frantic waterbugs. "Lighten up," Momma told me as I drove.

My mind was on the exit ahead where I would turn off onto a state highway, where the driving would go from punishment to pleasure. And as I made the turn, I said to her, "Now we'll see the real America!"

And we did. Along roads where woodlots still flank the ditchlines. Through crossroad hamlets. By the Frog Point Bar and Mel's Running Inn. Past neat farmyards where Herefords and Black Angus steers munched. Past oldtime farm houses with lightning rods and television antennas standing in incongruous mixture on their roofs; manure spreaders waiting by the barns, and the stars and stripes fluttering on silver flag poles on front lawns.

We slowed for small-town schools with their kids heading home; the boys swinging their jackets, the girls skipping along beneath their backpack school bags. Past a bridge repair crew that smiles and waves; and sideroad signs with names like "Long Ago Road" and "Plum Valley Road." A local radio station played real country music.

And the knot inside me began to unravel. I'd found my real America again.

- - - - - -

"Miz Spring, where are you?" I wondered as we rolled. And suddenly, there she was.

She'd crept in quietly, unnoticed. Yet there she stood, bedecked in an outfit of pale green trimmed with a necklace of red tulips and yellow daffodils, the sunshine sparkling in her eyes.

Lord, she was beautiful. And in my mind I embraced her.

- - - - - -

Two days on the road, and our destination; Kimberling City nestled in the timbered rugged hills of southwest Missouri, the heart of the scenic Ozarks. Home of sprawling Table Rock Lake with its 857 miles of shoreline and ten pound bass. Home of the White River, world famous for its brown and rainbow trout.

And the home of Wes and June Wight, our hosts.

- - - - - -

Branson, Missouri is a nearby tourist center. Branson has

become a mini-Nashville, a mecca for country music fans. The big-name performers come to its theaters. Drive through town and you'll see names like Roy Clark, George Jones, Reba McEntire, and Box Car Willie.

We took in a show, the Presley Mountain Music Jubilee -- two hours of banjo plucking, fiddle playing, gospel singing and slapstick comedy. Solid family fun. Good down-home, made-in-America style entertainment.

- - - - - -

The view from the Wight's deck was spectacular. In the foreground laid an arm of Table Rock Lake. In the background, cloaked in blue haze, rose the Ozarks. Hills with names like Bread Tray Mountain and Naked Joe Bald.

Surrounding their place, the woods was resplendent with the blooms of lavendar redbuds and white dogwood trees. And over all of it, hung the subtle soft hue of the hardwoods coming into leaf.

Miz Spring had certainly passed this way.

- - - - - -

But vacations come to an end. And as the trip was reversed, north we moved. Over the long causeways across the Harry Truman Reservoir, a tribute to one of my favorite people. Past the craft and gift shops where Momma paused for some last minute knickknacks. Lunch at the Red Rooster Inn at Polo, Missouri, population 683, the restaurant decorated in a chicken motif that almost flipped her.

- - - - - -

And home. The front yard snow bank had disappeared I noted as I opened the car door and got out. And there stood Miz Spring, smiling, dancing in the warm breeze.

"Ah seen ya'll down south a piece and ah've been awaiten' fer ya!" she whispered. And with that, she danced away; gone on her journey once more.

Lordy, but she's beauitiful!

May, 1989

# Fusion In A Jar

I've been reading lately about some highly scientific work going on out in Utah. Fusion in a jar, it's called.

Not being highly scientific, it goes a long way over my head. But as I understand the situation, the Utah boys take plutonium and mix it with something called heavy water. The result is supposed to be a new source of energy, sort of a mini atomic explosion.

Now, don't ask me what heavy water is. The only heavy water I've ever known was the stuff I used to carry in pails from the windmill when I was ten years old.

But the experiment has caused quite a ripple amongst highly scientific scientists. Imagine! A major breakthrough in high tech. Fusion in a jar!

Big deal! I've known about fusion in jars for over fifty years. And in jugs, bottles, and pots and pans.

Those highly scientific folks should come to Wisconsin. Wisconsin has been a leader in fusion in jars as long as I can remember. They could learn a few things about fusion.

Take one of my uncles, for instance. He created fusion in bottles back in the 30's, back in the Prohibition days. I remember the experiment real well.

Old Unk, it seems, got tired of paying black-market prices for his beer, weak stuff with no punch. And he decided to do something about it.

So he did a little research, consulting with his colleagues on how to make home-brew. Seems like there was a lot of that kind of highly scientific work going on in those days. The basic formula and the necessary laboratory equipment weren't hard to come by.

Well, Unk whipped up a batch, using of course, the highly scientific formula. I think he used the family bathtub as his test tube.

Now, I'll tell you he was proud of himself. The stuff, he thought, came out perfect. And into a collection of brown bottles he poured the luscious liquid, applying a bottle cap to each with one of those old-fashioned bottle cap presses.

Then down to the cellar he carried his loot, carefully storing it in a dark corner to age. Well, it didn't take long. Talk about fusion! Come the middle of the night, fusion really took place. One by one, the bottles blew up, almost rocking the house from its foundation.

Let me give you another example of Wisconsin fusion in a jar.

One cold winter day years ago, I was sitting around a campfire out in the woods having lunch with a bunch of loggers. There we squatted, toasting sandwiches on forked sticks over the red-hot coals. About ten of us.

Well, in the gang was a young forester fresh out of forestry school. And freshly married, I might add. As we sat there, shooting the bull, and munching our baloney, the young guy reached into his packsack and pulled out a jar; a jar containing some kind of a brown chocolately concoction, his dessert.

Young Guy turned the jar around in his fingers a couple times studying its contents. And he handed the jar to the logger next to him. "How about some dessert?" he asked. "Gee, thanks! I'm full," came the answer.

Around the circle, Young Guy passed the jar, asking each of us if we'd like the dessert. Noone accepted, one by one we turned him down; the last man handing it back to him.

"Aw, come on fellas!" he cried out in exasperation. "If I take it home, she'll cry!"

We knew fusion in a jar when we saw it, let me tell you. Another case.

Back in my boyhood fishing days, bullheads were big. Over to a crick or a river I'd hike with my pole to catch bullheads.

Well, being somewhat on the highly scientific side when it came to fishing, I'd read in one of my outdoor scientific journals about "stink" bait. Make some good stink bait and you'll really catch bullheads.

So I did. I stole a pint mason jar from the fruit cellar, and I went about making me some stink bait. In went a handful of hefty worms, then a chunk of old cheese and a few leftover chicken parts from out by the woodpile.

Mix it all up good; seal the jar and set it out in the hot sun for a couple days, the instructions said. You'll have yourself some good stink bait.

I did.

Wow! Talk about fusion in a jar! When I opened that baby up, there'd been fusion all right.

Utah can't hold a candle to Wisconsin when it comes to fusion.

May, 1989

# Love For The Land

From the highway, the old farm field north of Trego looks like all abandoned farm fields in northern Wisconsin this time of year... drab, covered with brown weeds and grass. But look closely, and one can see more. Rows of trees line the old plot's surface, leafless hardwood trees, standing like spindly sticks in neat rows, obviously planted trees.

They're black walnut trees. And that's what makes the plantation different, unique. Black walnut trees aren't supposed to grow well in northern Wisconsin. Oh, once in awhile one or two are found growing in a front yard. But not several acres of black walnuts growing in a neat, well-tended plantation. Plantings such as those are normally reserved for the fertile soils of the southern part of the state, where walnut trees are native.

The trees and the land belong to Fred and Lucille Bohne, retired folks from Chicago where Fred worked as a railroad engineer. Now 76 and 74 years old respectively, the Bohnes bought the 200 acre idle farm in 1968. From their kitchen of the home overlooking tiny Blue Lake, just down the slope of the lawn, they can watch otters play at the water's edge, and eagles soar overhead.

"We're keeping the property pretty much as a nature preserve," Fred told me. "This farm doesn't have one square foot of level ground on it. And we're letting it go into woods."

Shielding the front of the house is a pole-size stand of red pines, planted by the previous owner. The Bohnes have watched the trees grow from tiny seedlings, prompting them to plant more pines and even some tamaracks.

But their walnut trees are their special interest.

"We have two mature walnut trees on the property," Lucille explained. "The one in the front yard produces nuts, and we thought 'let's plant 'em!' "

And so, without professional forestry guidance, the Bohnes began their experimentation with walnut trees, growing their own seedlings for planting.

The nuts, Fred explained, are placed in furrows made with his tractor, planted a few inches deep into the soil. "Just deep enough to discourage squirrels from digging them up," he says.

Planted in the fall, the nuts remain in their "seed beds" over winter. "The nuts have to freeze to germinate," he noted.

And come spring, the nuts do grow, sending up stems and leaves. Growing rapidly, the seedlings reach heights of a foot by late June. It's then that the Bohnes transplant the young trees.

"If you leave them too long, they'll get a long tap root," they said. "We're careful to protect the roots. We shade them with wet cloths. We plant them in rows eight feet apart with the seedlings six feet apart in the rows."

The best soil for walnuts is a rocky clay, Fred said. "We're the poorest place in the world for soil to grow farm crops, but the trees grow good."

For a short time, Bohne cultivated the walnut trees with his tractor. However, soil erosion from rain storms forced

*Black walnut trees were planted by Lucille and Fred Bohne.*

him to abandon that practice, though the trees did grow better.

To date, the Bohnes have planted 4,000 walnut seedlings, the oldest now eight years old and almost twelve feet tall. As they grow, Lucille trims the side branches with a hedge shears.

"I trim them every year so they grow right," she says. A clear trunk allows the tree to grow into high quality lumber and veneer logs.

Their children and grandchildren come home periodically to visit and to help with the work. "The kids have helped a lot," Lucille commented.

And what rewards do the Bohnes receive for their efforts?

"We feel it's making our property more valuable," Fred said. "It's an investment in our land. And there's the satisfaction of seeing them grow."

"It's good exercise," Lucille added. "And it's fun."

Right now, resting in seed beds on a nearby rocky slope are 2,000 black walnut seedlings. And next summer those young trees are scheduled for transplanting.

Of course, all the forestry books say that walnuts aren't suitable for northern Wisconsin.

However, nobody's told that to Fred and Lucille Bohne.

...Fortunately!

December, 1992

# Home Is Where The Heat Is!

It's six o'clock in the morning, and I'm driving south on U.S. 53, headed for a meeting at Stevens Point. I'm alone, just me and my faithful pickup truck friend, rolling together down the highway.

Outside, the pitch black morning is cold. I know that. But how cold? I switch on the radio, catch some music on the Rice Lake station, and Dick Kaner tells me that it's thirteen below, a nice round figure for a January morning in northern Wisconsin.

Inside the cab, the heater is running full blast, doing its best to fight off the crusts of icy frost that keep trying to creep in from the edges of the windshield. What's the wind chill, I wonder, of a truck travelling at 55 miles an hour when it's thirteen below? Close to a hundred below probably, cold enough to cause mechanical troubles, something I don't need on a deserted highway.

So I'm prepared. I've thought ahead. Alongside me on the seat, rest my insulated ice fishing pants. Dirty, cruddy, but there--to serve me if I need them. And in the storage box, rests a pair of felt-lined boots and a bulky hooded coat, so oversized that it will slip over the jacket I'm wearing. When it comes to winter travel in Wisconsin, I'm no dummy! I come ready for the worst.

Over the past forty years, there's been a ton of winter driving--on business, to distant relatives and friends for holidays, weddings, funerals, and what not all. Trips that sometimes went well. And sometimes didn't--turning into tense, scary, dangerous experiences.

Like the return trip home from a Christmas visit to Momma's folks many years ago. Late at night, I was on the last leg from Antigo to Tomahawk. Things had gone well, uneventful. Alongside me, Momma slumped, asleep. On the back seat the two kids snoozed. Under Momma's feet, Sport, the family springer spaniel, snored. All was peaceful.

And then, out of nowhere, the snowstorm to end all snowstorms. Down it dumped, huge fluffy flakes, a curtain of white; eye-boggling, almost hypnotic in the headlights. Visibility was barely fifty feet, roadsides and ditches totally obscured.

Fortunately, ahead of me somewhere was another vehicle, leaving two faint tire tracks in the snow rapidly building on the road. And by following that dim trail, I managed to limp to U.S. 51, and home.

Travelling with a family in winter can be touchy.

And another memorable adventure, a bitter cold night back in the late 70's.

Dave Jacobson and I were headed for a meeting at Brule. Dave was DNR's district director, and one of the perks of his position was a personally assigned state automobile. Only his was a real beater, an old semi-compact four cylinder job with a speedometer loaded with miles.

We knew the weather conditions. And we knew the forecast before we left home--temperatures far below zero, high winds, drifting snow! Absolutely dangerous conditions! Common sense said to stay home. But we didn't.

And as we headed north from Hayward on Highway 27

into the Eau Claire Lakes country, the full fury of the storm hit us. Dave fought to keep the old heap on the road, the wind pummelling the car with icy blasts, its headlights barely piercing the raging blizzard.

We'd come prepared. In the back seat laid heavy boots and insulated clothing. Yet, even they might not suffice were we to stall on the desolate road. Both of us were concerned, tight-lipped, aware of what was on each of our minds. And suddenly, breaking the silence, a typical Jacobson decision.

"You know what we're going to do it we get hung up out here," he said half question-like. "We'll tough it out as long as we can. And then we're going to set this (bleepity-bleep) state car on fire!"

And he would have.

......It's almost seven o'clock at night. I'm on the last miles home from the day in Stevens Point, and the pickup's performing perfectly. Outside it's eight below zero, the radio says; still mighty cold. Another winter travel trip is about to end. I've made it again, and I breathe a grateful sigh.

Home, they say, is where the HEART is. I say it's where the HEAT is... in January... in northern Wisconsin.

January, 1991

# Bill's Birthday Party

I went to a birthday party the other day... Bill Kauffman's. Bill turned 86 recently, and his family held a little get-together, inviting some of his friends to stop by and help him celebrate.

I've known Bill for quite a few years now. His son, Willie, grades my roads and plows my snow out at the Christmas tree farm. So when I'm driving by, like in the summer when I'm on my way trout fishing, I stop at their Springbrook home to say hello and shoot a little breeze.

Bill had a nice party the other day. Quiet, laid back, just the kind of an affair we old duffers enjoy. Six of us were there, counting Bill, but not counting grandkids and great grandkids and a couple of other folks who happened to come by.

Morris and Viola Anderson were there, for instance. Morris is an old pal of Bill's. He's 86 too, though a couple months younger, which makes a difference when you're 86. Morris, in his younger days, was a practical veterinarian, using skills he learned from his father to treat cows and horses, like Bill's, many years ago.

Morris sat through the party in his wheelchair, confined there by a stroke he suffered a year or so ago. That didn't stop him from having a good time, however.

Ralph Allar was there. Ralph's 90 now. Lives around the

corner from Bill a ways, up near Springbrook where he ran a garage and welding shop back in the 1930's. He told some good tales about those times. He uses a stout cane these days, but he gets around very well.

Floyd Moyer came. Floyd's a chipper mere 81. He lives up the road, a few miles north of Stone Lake, a place he's called home since he was 24 years old. Except for six years when he was a logger out west. His home's just a couple mail boxes from my Stone Lake tree farm. And we visited about the area, as he remembers it from years ago.

Jerry Hanacek was there. He was the kid in the bunch, only 66; what some old-timers might call a young whipper-snapper. Jerry ran a machine shop in Trego for many years, building the best winches and jammers for logging skidders in the country. Listen to him talk about how he built his machines, avoiding half-twists in the cables which cause the wire to fray, and you just know he was good at his trade.

Last there was myself, a crotchety sixty-something senior, not known for much of anything... except possibly not knowing much of anything.

The six of us sat around in Bill's living room, letting the talk flow, enjoying the humor that comes out of stories about life years ago. I asked Floyd if he knew about the old Edgewood school that once stood near my property. He sure did, he said, went there as a boy. And he told how a new kid came to school one day, and he and Floyd got into a rassling match. Well, the new kid had a quarter in his pocket, which got lost, which was a small fortune to a kid back in those days.

Ralph told how he used to make his own acetelyne gas for his cutting torch in the 30's, a mite on the dangerous side if you weren't careful. And he told about the old cars that had carbide headlights. Each headlight had to be lit individually with a match, he said. But they threw a good light. To that Bill, Morris and Floyd all agreed, especially if you kept the reflectors properly shined, they said.

Somebody mentioned moonshining. Was there much going on, I asked. After all, Prohibition and the Depression went hand in hand. Quite a bit, they said. You could tell who made it by holding a glassful up to the light. One maker used iodine to color his, others used brown sugar. And the talk took me back to my own boyhood when my grandfather would point out a woods where the revenuers had raided a still, leaving the ground littered with smashed shiny cans.

The subject got on railroads, Floyd telling how a man he knew modified his bicycle so he could ride the Soo Line's rails into Stone Lake. And Jerry told of the time he and a friend got overtaken by a train in a tunnel out west. How they squeezed into holes in the rock walls to avoid being killed.

About then, Content, Bill's granddaughter, called that the food was on. Over to the table we went to load up on ham sandwiches, potato chips and cheese, all topped off with birthday cake and chocolate-swirl ice cream.

Last, Bill opened his presents, helped by one of his great-granddaughters. He got some warm socks, a pair of fleece-lined gloves, some jockey shorts and two dandy flannel shirts. Just the kind of stuff an 86-year-old likes and needs. Each gift had a nice card, which Bill read but kept to himself. What they said, after all, was none of our business. Which is only right.

And then, we went home.

It was a good birthday party. We should have another one just like it next year, I say.

December, 1994

# Soderbeck Ferry

Behind him, in the background, as Bill Soderbeck talked, the St. Croix River surged and swirled, powerfully, as it slid southward on its journey to join the Mississippi. Soderbeck, now 78, was talking, about the lifetime he's spent on the banks of the river. And I listened... fascinated by his words.

"I was born right over there," Bill said, pointing into the woods on the Minnesota side. "My folks had a farm there. There were fourteen of us kids, eight boys and six girls. I've lived all of my life within a mile of where I was born."

I'd met Bill earlier at the homestead tucked in the pines and oaks west of Grantsburg where he and Alice, his wife now live. He was busy in his garden, tending the peas that were in bloom and the tomatos just beginning to blossom.

And together we drove the backwoods roads that would lead us to the river. "These roads were just one-lane trails back in the 1920's," he said. "Nothing but two ruts. Those old cars back then had high wheels. You could put them in the ruts and take your hands off the steering wheel until you came to a crossroad!"

A rustic, neatly-routed brown sign caught my eye as we passed. "Soderbeck's Ferry Landing," it said, our destination.

Now located on lands of the National Park Service, the old ferry crossing is being preserved as a historic site. And well it should be. For a colorful period of our past; of the Soderbeck family, the river, and society in general of the region, has transpired there.

"Dad put in his first ferry in 1922," Bill began. "It worked, but in 1927 he built a bigger one, all of Washington fir. He built it upside down, and we kids helped turn it over with A-frames and winches. It was 36 feet long and 16 feet wide."

Soderbeck has made a scale model of that old boat. And with it, he demonstrated how it worked, how the hinged ends allowed it to be loaded.

"Dad's first load in 1927 was a circus," Bill continued. "A Fordson tractor with steel wheels pulling a big trailer with an elephant in it. And some horses! It was a heavy load!"

"After that we had other circuses too. But the elephants were always walked across the river by their trainers. The elephants liked the water so much they didn't want to get out of the river."

The ferry boat was controlled by a large overhead cable anchored to both riverbanks. The boat rode at an angle in the water, allowing the current to provide the power to push it across. "When we had enough water," Bill said. "When the water was low, we used manpower to pull it across hand-over-hand on a second smaller cable."

The river crossing served as a focal point for the humanity of the 1920's and 1930's. It operated until 1943. A trip across the river cost fifty cents.

"Farmers hauled their wheat across to the flour mill in Grantsburg," Soderbeck told. "And Indian families passed through to pick rice in Minnesota."

"We saw lots of Gypsy caravans. They'd come in eight or ten big touring cars. The guys and girls would jump right in

*Bill Soderbeck displays a model of the ferry boat his father once operated on the St. Croix River.*

the river. There'd always be one truck with curtains on the sides. In it, rode the Gypsy lady who was the boss of the group, smoking a big cigar. She had all the money.

Sometimes there'd be some haggling with Dad over payment."

"Bootleggers too. Those were Prohibition days. One day a guy driving a Model B Ford Coupe stopped. It had two gas tanks and overload springs, obviously for running moonshine. One of the gas tanks was leaking, and he asked if we could fix it. Well, my brother did, but sixty gallons of alcohol had to be unloaded from the trunk first."

Bill Soderbeck told me a lot more. Stories of the sawmill his father ran, of logging in the winters in below zero weather pulling a crosscut saw. Of the deadheads they salvaged from the river, big pine logs up to 36 feet long that had been lost on the river drives years earlier, when the old-time lumberjacks logged the virgin timber along the St. Croix.

Of back-country farmers that starved out when their thin sandy soil gave out. Of long-gone trappers that lived all winter in tents, shooting snowshoe rabbits for food. Of his mother using fifty pounds of flour a week to bake bread and pancakes for the family.

And he told of the days before World War II when engineers came to survey the river, to take cores from its bottom, data for dams that might be built, dams that would have stilled the St. Croix's spirit and erased Soderbeck's Ferry Landing.

Bill Soderbeck looks back now at those times and the river that's been so much a part of his life.

"Keep it the way it is," he said to me the other day.

And I couldn't agree more.

July, 1993

# Charlie Cool Takes A Trip

Well, Charlie Cool, my not-yet-two grandson has been galavanting around the country again. This time he flew the friendly skies out to Maine to see his Grandma Polly.

Actually his real name is Kyle. But I've called him Charlie Cool ever since he started to display his laid-back personality. I suppose he was about six months old.

Grandfathers have had the right to give their grandsons nicknames for a long time. That authority is spelled out in the grandfathers' bill of rights, rights declared several thousand years ago by a counsel of cavemen grandfathers. Rights they carved with a sharp rock on the wall of a cave on a mountain-side in southeast Mesopatamia.

Some years back an old archeologist discovered the cave and after long and deliberate study diciphered the ancient writings. There it was, plain as day. "Article Six: Forever hereafter, be it known to all mankind that grandfathers hereby have the inalienable right to bestow upon their grandsons any and all titles deemed appropriate to recognize said grandsons' distinct and unique characters."

The old archeologist, being a grandfather himself, immediately recognized the importance of his discovery. And fearing exploitation of his find by a less-than-understanding world, sealed the cave. The secret has been shared only by confidential word of mouth amongst grandfathers ever since.

Back to Charlie's trip.

Momma and I went up to Hayward the day before he and his mom were to depart. Charlie was his usual self, taking it all in stride, tossing his rubber ball around the living room, doing somersaults on the rug.

But Charlie's into tractors. And as we stood in the yard lingering with our final farewell, he toddled over to the closed garage door and gave its handle a good pull. "Stuck!" he said turning to his dad. Inside was his favorite toy, the riding lawn mower.

Well, his plea tugged at heart strings and up the door was rolled. Over to the lawn tractor Charlie goes and gives the starter rope a couple of good yanks. "Tractor-r-r! Tractor-r-r!" he pleaded. No choice, Dad had to start the tractor.

And as Momma and I eased down the driveway in the pickup; there was Charlie on his dad's lap, tooling along beside us in low gear, a smile from ear lobe to ear lobe, too busy to even wave a bye-bye.

Well, the trip out east went well. Charlie's a seasoned traveler. Airport terminal crowds and ticket counters don't phase him. Oh, the take-offs and landings bothered his ears some. I'm not surprised. I've always known he's had sensitive ears. They've never missed anything.

But when the pretty stewardesses begin to gather round him, oohing and aahing over his red hair and dimples, and fastening their flight wings pin on his new Oshkosh B'Gosh bib overalls; he settles right in.

This trip he had the chance to sit next to a couple of middle-aged businessmen. Odds are that they were grandfathers too. Charlie turned on his charms, and in a matter of minutes he was sitting on their laps, smearing crumbs and frosting from his cookie on their fancy three-piece $500 suits.

And when his embarrassed mom desparately tried to apologize, the good old boys would have no part of it. "Leave us alone. We're having a conference!" they told her in no uncertain terms.

I saw some pictures of Charlie's visit the other day, photos taken with Grandma Polly and the others. There he stood, poised, hands in his pockets, right at home. And I heard the tales of the live lobsters cooked for supper and the brook trout that his Uncle Dale caught to show him.

But the best photo of all was the one of Charlie standing beaming next to a big green and yellow John Deere tractor, a tractor for Maine's potato fields, a tractor with chains on its huge rubber-tired wheels. Charlie was in his glory.

Well, all good visits come to an end. And finally Charlie's trip home. There waiting for him at the gate at the Minneapolis airport was his dad. "Daddy! Daddy!" he called from halfway down the ramp.

Three hours later, asleep in his car seat, at midnight he was home. And as his dad lifted him from the backseat, he half-opened his eyes, looked around in the darkness, and murmured, "Tractor-r-r! Tractor-r-r!"

No, there'd be no midnight tractor ride and into his jammies he was tucked. But as the bedroom door was softly closed, one last half-whispered plea.

"Tractor-r-r!"

May, 1988

# Shearing Christmas Trees

"Snip! Snip! Snip!" the hedge clippers snap, and the green pine boughs fall to the ground. Shearing Christmas trees is a tedious task.

Finish a tree, turn around, and there's another looking at you, needing a haircut.

"Bzzz! Bzzz! Bzzz!" the deer flies buzz, taking aim at my ears, as I bend to trim a whorl of ragged branches from the trunk of a tree.

"Slap! Slap! Slap!" my hands clap as I try to swat the little boogers. But they're too quick for me, and the welts on my ears swell and itch.

"Drip! Drip! Drip!" drops the sweat from my brow as I work, methodically plodding my way along the rows of trees. And "Glug! Glug! Glug!" sounds the water jug when at last I treat myself to a break.

Shearing Christmas trees is a hot, dirty, thirst-filled job.

Why is it, I ask myself, that pine trees need to be trimmed at the hottest time of the year? There's a reason, of course. Unlike the more sensible spruces and firs, pines produce buds only at the tips of their twigs.

The Christmas tree grower knows this. He knows his white, norway and scotch pines must be sheared the latter part of June, in the growing season. Only then can the tender new shoots be trimmed back; so a rosette of new buds will form, buds that will burst and grow the next year to produce a symetrical tree.

The more sensible spruces and firs, Mother Nature made them the way trees were supposed to be made, with buds all along their branches. Internodal buds, the scientists call them. So, spruces and firs can be sheared any time -- like on nice cool days. When it's fun to be outdoors.

And why shape the trees in the first place? Well, the tree grower knows full well that come December, most of us will be out searching for the perfect Christmas tree, one that'll look just right glowing by the living room window.

But Christmas trees are like people, all individuals. Sure, a few fortunates are so handsome that they're chosen to grace governors' mansions, even the White House. But they're rare, like the handful of beautiful people with faces and bodies so special that Hollywood puts them on film.

And, like people, Christmas trees have their problems. I see their troubles as I move through the plantation. Here's one missing, a gap where a seedling didn't make it, its roots chewed off by grubs. One with a dead top, its leader killed by tip weevils. Another with a red-brown side branch infected with blister rust. And a lopsided tree, nipped by a hungry deer.

Why do I do it, I say to myself! Why go through all this work and strife? And I don't have a real good answer. The best I can come up with is that I'm a son of the soil, an old farm boy who still likes to watch green things grow.

"Rumble! Rumble! Rumble!" grumbles the thunder. I look to the west where the white billowy clouds are building, their undersides already turning to blue-black. I'd appreciate the rain -- the young trees need it. But the job has to get done. Time is running out.

The first drops spatter against the brim of my straw hat. I hurry to do a few more trees. But the storm catches me, and I retreat to the truck.

The downpour drums on the roof, splashes on the windshield, as I watch the storm move up the Namekagon Valley. Jagged, white-hot streaks of lightning stab at the earth. Thunder echoes across the wooded hills like artillery fire.

Head for home; call it a day? I decide not. There's no show on the tube that can compare with the one I'm watching. And I light my pipe and settle back.

Past the front of the truck, oblivious to the rain; a pair of tree swallows, residents of one of my bluebird houses, dart through the air; capturing insects to feed their hungry young. There's a lesson there, I decide. There's no thought on their part of giving up, of quitting.

An orange-black Monarch butterfly flits from one purple clover head to another, sipping nectar, unconcerned. Come Fall, those same fragile wings will flutter all the way to Mexico or South America. A wood tick crawls along my pant leg, and a mosquitoe hums overhead.

And it's then that I begin to understand.

The swallows, the butterfly, the wood tick, the mosquitoe, the rain and lightning, I decide, are there because they're supposed to be, doing what they must.

And so it is with me.

July, 1989

# Lone Pine School

Lone Pine... a great name for a country school if I ever heard one!

Lone Pine School... I can see the old classroom now, a single tall white pine standing in its yard silhouetted against the morning sky, a beacon beckoning to country youngsters as they marched along country roads... the notes of a clanging bell echoing softly across the countryside announcing that another day of learning was about to begin.

Located just north of Shell Lake, off on a side road, the old school still stands. But today its mission has changed. Now it's the Beaver Brook town hall. And its business consists of town matters, not teaching farm kids reading, writing and arithmetic.

Arnold Hess and I visited the Lone Pine school recently. Arnold is 82 now, born nearby on a farm carved by his parents in the early 1900's from brush land that remained after the virgin forest had been cut over. "I began the first grade in 1916 when I was five years old," he told me. "It was a mile-and-a-half from my home to the school, and I walked that every morning and night. A good part of it was through the woods. That was quite a thing for a five-year-old!"

Hess remembers well the eight years he attended Lone Pine, including the names of his teachers. "Jennie Schricker was my first and second grade teacher," he reminisced.

*Arnold Hess attended the Lone Pine School. A stump remains of the tree that gave the school its name.*

"Mary Olson third grade, Florence Huntley fourth, Josie Harrington fifth and sixth, and Irma Cable for seventh and eighth. My sister Hildegarde taught there too in the 1930's. I hiked over every day to build the fire for her."

Arnold went on to explain how the local community in

those early times had many people of German heritage, including his parents. German was the language commonly spoken.

"My sister, Della, only spoke and understood German," he told. "And she almost drove the teachers crazy. Finally my mother said, 'From now on, it'll only be English spoken here at home. ' "

Attendance at Lone Pine averaged about 25 students a year for its eight grades. "A class of five kids was a big class," Arnold noted. "The younger children learned a lot by listening in on the older kids. All the kids could read, write and do arithmetic."

"We even had hot lunches," he continued. "The school had a little two-burner kerosene stove that smoked like heck. We kids would take turns bringing food, and the teacher would do the cooking. The older girls peeled the spuds and helped. We had vegetable soup, beef stew, and milk and potatoes... I just loved that!"

I asked about conduct. "The teachers had discipline," he replied. "They didn't allow the kids to get wild. It also came from home. My dad said, 'The teacher's the boss. If you get in trouble in school, you'll be in trouble here at home.' "

Look at the old school building today, and one finds windows only on its east side. "I remember when someone got the brilliant idea to not have windows on the west side," he said. "So they boarded up that side and put those windows with those on the east. After that, we always had a shadow. But they never changed them back because they didn't want to admit they were wrong."

Dress was simple, he said. "Nothing fancy. Longjohns to keep us warm on our walks to school, bib overalls for the boys, long dresses for the girls. They didn't wear slacks then."

Programs were put on in the fall at Halloween, at Christmas, and in the spring at Easter. "Those were big events for the parents," he said.

What about the play at recesses, I asked as we stood talking on the old school ground.

"We played games like pom-pom-pullaway and hide and seek. I remember when we were given a football. We didn't know what to do with it. And later we got a basketball. Of course, we didn't have a basket!" he chuckled.

"And right here where it was level we played baseball."

"Back in those days, kids could have fun without spending a dime. Today I see kids laying ten dollar bills down in stores. If I'd have had ten dollars as a boy, I'd have been a millionaire!"

Then too, Arnold Hess told me more than tales about his old-time school.

How the big sawmill in Shell Lake employed 700 men, shipping 25 rail cars of lumber a day, from logs cut from pine forests where his father worked. How his father, accustomed to driving horses, drove his first car, a Model T Ford, into a shed and yelled "Whoa!" to stop it. How covered wagons served as school buses.

Beautiful stories all... of how life once was for Arnold Hess.

May, 1993

# Hazards Of High-Tech

Well, folks, Momma and I have gone high-tech. We're into computers now. No longer do we have to hang our heads and look dejectedly at the floor when someone says, "You mean you haven't got a computer!" No longer do we have to feel that we're a couple old fogies that can't keep up with the times.

Yup! Parked along one wall of a spare bedroom; glistening in brand-new, factory-fresh white, rest a mainframe, a keyboard and color monitor, a printer and all the other lessor doodads that go with these latest of modern-day rages. Banished to a tabletop off to the side is the "old" electric typewriter that was "new" just a year or two ago.

Yup! We've taken that giant leap forward for mankind. And it's an exciting new ballgame.

Momma's worked as a secretary in the past. Today, she does all of my typing. Without her help, few words would end up on paper.

"Boy," she'd said several times this past year, "would I like a computer. Would I ever enjoy working on one of those!"

So I bought her one of the new-fangled gadgets. And for the past month, she's been learning to use it. With some help of course. For example, she signed up for a course over at the high school. There she picked up the basics.

Then, over Christmas, we had our daughter, and family home. All are pretty good on computers. But let me tell you, it's kind of scary to watch an eight-year-old giving instructions to his grandma on what keys to punch. One quickly gets a clearer understanding of what's meant by "generation gap."

So she's coming along, gaining in confidence. I sit beside her as she types and marvel as the words miraculously appear on the monitor screen. I watch as she edits in changes, slips a little black plastic disk into a slot, and presses a button. The nearby printer begins to clickity-clack, and out streams a finished copy of a story.

No longer is there the hesitancy, the fear that should she hit the wrong key, smoke will start billowing from the software porthole.

Not that there aren't moments. Take the other day for instance. Smoothly, professionally, she'd typed a column for me. A few editing alterations; a comma here, a spelling correction there, and the thing was ready for printing.

"Save!" she told the machine, meaning that the story was to be stored on one of those little black disks. Yellow and green instructions flickered on the screen. Everything seemed to be compatible, as they say in the computer trade.

"Print!" she ordered with a flourish of her forefinger. And like a buck private saluting his commanding officer, the printer snapped to attention, its heels clicking in obedience. I could read the look on her face, the satisfied smile from wielding such immense power. Everything was going fine. Right?

Wrong! The printer began its clickity-clacking, but out spits a story from the week before. Back up, try again, and the same thing. For four hours she struggled with the mutinous monster. But to no avail.

"I'm a failure," she said, giving up. "I'll try again tomorrow."

The crack of dawn the next morning found her back on the job, the room silent as she pored over her manuals. And finally success; out prints the right story.

I was proud of her, really proud. And I poured myself a cup of coffee and picked up my big-town morning paper. "Oh no!" I gasped.

There on the front page in bold headlines was the news that AT & T, the American Telephone and Telegraph Company, had suffered a major computer breakdown the day before. Across the country, long distance telephone calls had been disrupted.

Was it a coincidence? Or had Momma punched a wrong button? Maybe I had one of those "hackers" on my hands. You know, one of those people who get sadistic kicks from infecting computer programs with "viruses," causing the tinny think tanks to get sick and blow their lids.

Frankly, I'm worried. AT & T's a big outfit. I sure don't want to get on the wrong side of AT & T. I like AT & T. They have nice telephone girls that always tell me to have a nice day when I make my long distance calls.

So I'm watching the mail. So far, I haven't received any nasty letters from AT & T's legal boys threatening to send me to Sing Sing.

I've got my fingers crossed -- that Momma didn't get her wires crossed.

February, 1990

# Meet The Quarter-Pounder!

Russia, you've had it!

No, I'm not talking about all the political hassling that's going on, or the unrest that's boiling over. I'm not talking about places like Poland and East Germany that have quit the team. Those are just minor little things.

I'm talking about MacDonald's coming to Moscow. When you let those golden arches come to town, you opened up a mighty big can of cheeseburgers let me tell you.

Sure, it was a nice little gesture. Open up a little. Lighten up a little. Let a little of that decadent capitalism come in. So what? What harm can it do? Well, don't say I didn't warn you!

For most of my life, I've listened to the running battle of propaganda about the respective virtues of communism and capitalism. I heard your old chief, Nikita Kruschev, extoll "We will bury you?" Old Nikita meant in tractors from the assembly lines of his glorious five-year plans.

Now it's your turn! We will bury you -- in French fries!

Having lived through the evolution of the fast-food industry here in the good old U.S., I figure I'm in a pretty good position to judge. I saw the drive-in go from a cozy little Frostop where families went on hot summer nights for nickel root beers, to the computerized cash registers Hardee's gals now punch to ring up my order of quarter-pounders.

Get ready! You're about to be blitzed like you've never been blitzed before, with flip-top styrofoam hamburger boxes and plastic tubes of catsup and mustard. Extras of which your wives will toss into the glove compartments of your cars and promptly forget. Tubes that will ooze and leak all over your road maps and sunglasses.

I've seen it. I know what I'm talking about.

Another thing.

I don't know how many '78 Chevies you've got on your used car lots. But you better check. If you're short, get busy and import a big batch. Out there somewhere lurking in the suburbs of Moscow is a horde of teenagers.

And they're going to want those old heaps. They're going to want to put big tires on them and raise the rearends a couple of feet with super-duper shock absorbers. They're going to want to hang foxtails on the rear view mirrors and stuffed Garfield cats from the back windows.

They're going to put four-barrel carburetors on those old jalops and shiny exhaust pipes underneath, pipes that will rattle the windows of the Kremlin when they cut out of the parking lot, after a strawberry milkshake, to cruise your babushka-clad chicks on Red Square!

Talk about culture shock! Are you ready for it?

Oh, I forgot something.

Get your local industrial development commission cranking. You're going to need a big shopping center right now. Maybe a K-Mart or two, places that sell gym shoes, the higher-priced the better. Don't mess with the cheapo brands. Those teenagers of yours aren't about to wear them. Figure on something in the 100 to 200 ruble range at least. And don't bother to teach your shoe clerks to lace them. The kids never do anyway.

And don't forget the stone-washed jeans, the baggy kind with the narrow cuffs. And the cool black sunglasses, ones like the Blues Brothers wear on television.

Then there's a little matter of discrimination. Now that you've let MacDonald's in, how about Burger King and Wendy's, Pizza Palace, Chicken Delight, and Taco John's? They deserve equal treatment, you know. Who knows, burritos might go over big after a couple hundred years of cabbage soup.

Your zoning committee better get off its bureaucratic butt too. You're gonna need a strip out on the edge of town where these joints can settle. What with all the bright neon signs flashing, it'll make a first-class tourist attraction. The glow at night might even brighten up Siberia a bit. I've heard Siberia can stand a little brightening.

Listen up! I don't pass on all this high-class wisdom and advice lightly. Mr. Gorbachev says there's gotta be change. All I'm saying is do some deep thinking before it's too late. Nothing brings change faster than a hamburger with everything.

I know. I speak from personal experience. My kids could say "MacDonald's" before they could say "da-da"!

February, 1990

# A Lifetime Of Horses

For an instant I couldn't believe my eyes. Yet there it was, a picture from the past, a scene taking me back in time.

The country road I was driving wound its way through woods and fields of rural Burnett County. And there, along a fence line, was a team of horses pulling an old-fashioned corn cultivator, the kind my grandfathers used many years ago.

This I had to see! And I pulled into a driveway, turned around, and headed back. And, I came to know Jim Kreutzian and Lawrence Nelson.

Kreutzian and Nelson are neighbors and avid horsemen, I learned. The big draft-work-animal kind that once plowed fields and pulled hay wagons before tractors become the source of power for farmers. What prompted that interest, that affection, I wondered.

I spent a pleasant evening with Jim and Lawrence; and Jim's wife, Eleanor, recently. We talked about horses, and why they own them. It's a hobby, they both said. Jim is 72 now, and Lawrence is 65. They've been around draft horses all their lives. Each own a team today, plus younger yearlings and colts.

"I grew up with horses," Jim told. "When I retired, I said I was going to have a team."

"He always said he wanted a big field of knee-high clover

where he could sit in an easy chair with his horses, his hound dog, and his pipe," Eleanor added. "Now he's got it all but the hound dog and the pipe."

"I've had horses almost all of my life," said Lawrence. "Since I got out of grade school. They're a peaceful animal."

And pictures from Eleanor's scrapbook of horses they've owned. "Our grandkids named them all," she said.

Both Jim and Lawrence belong to the Wisconsin Draft Horse and Mule Association, an organization here in the west-central part of the state that's perpetuating the nostalgia of horses. The group holds meetings each spring and fall.

"Lots of times there's a hundred or more horses," Jim said. "They come from all over." At the outings, horses are used to demonstrate how farm work was performed years ago.

"A lot of elderly people come to see how it was done when they were kids," Lawrence noted. "But a lot of the younger folks are also getting interested."

On September 25, starting at 10 am, such a field day will be held near Grantsburg. "On the old Pickle Factory Road," Eleanor explained. Old-time horse-powered farming methods like plowing, mowing, raking and threshing will be shown.

Then, Jim and Lawrence conduct hay rides in summer and sleigh rides in winter, once a week in early evening, with their teams and battery-lighted wagons, for young people. The youngsters are mainly members of youth and church groups.

"The kids are well-behaved," they said. "We have a heck of a time getting them on the wagons. They all have to pet the horses and feed them hay. They always have to learn their names and find out if they're boy or girl horses. And of

*Lawrence Nelson, Jim Kreutzian and his grandson, Jason Althoff, have a fondness for draft horses.*

course, some of them have to help drive. That's a thrill for them! They enjoy that!"

"Some groups sing a lot. You can hear them all the way to Grantsburg," they said.

I learned a lot more the other night. Things like how harnesses are getting scarce. "The old ones are getting hard to find," Jim said. "They've been drug out of all the old barns." And how the two men now depend on Amish farmers near Pine City, Minnesota for their harness repairs. And their blacksmithing needs.

I watched as Jim placed bridles on his team, Sally and Prince, speaking softly to them. "Whoa! Get over there! Back up!"

I listened to the mellow, musical "clip-clop" of their hoofs as they pranced along the blacktop pavement.

Then, I stood in silent satisfaction as young city kids pet-ted the faces of Arnie and Katie, real live horses, chattering excitedly to the experience.'

And I was taken back to my own youth, to sights and sounds I once knew, to memories revived by two men with a deep love for horses.

It felt good to be there.

September, 1993

# Don't Call Me . . . I'll Call You!

"Why don't you give Nancy a call?" I said matter-of-factly. And with that Momma picked up the phone, punched in some numbers, and waited for her friend to answer.

Now, making a phone call these days is no big deal. We all make them, lots of them. But this call was different. Momma and I were rolling along the highway north of Rice Lake in the pickup. And hanging from a little patch of Velcro on the dashboard was my newest toy, a cellular telephone.

"Hi, there!" I heard Momma say. And I breathed a sigh of relief. The gadget works, I thought to myself. Coming from the days of kerosene lamps and horses and wagons, I'm always distrustful of new-fangled gadgets with a lot of buttons.

"You'll never guess where I'm calling you from," Momma went on. "I'm in the truck out on the highway. We just had a phone put in. And you're the first call we've made!"

And so a new chapter in a lifetime of experiences with telephones is being written. Here I'm barely used to walking around the house with one of those fancy cordless jobs... and now I can talk to anyone in the country while I'm tooling down a firelane.

Amazing!

Telephones and I go back a long way together. Hey! I can

remember when my farm neighborhood got all excited because a telephone line was being built along the town road. Cedar poles, two green glass insulators at their tops, and two wires that hummed in the breeze.

Not that the line did most of us much good. Back in those depression-day times very few folks could afford to "hook on." Still, the line looked nice, kind of a status symbol to poor country folks.

And as my brother and I gradually figured out how telephones worked, we tried making our own. Someone, probably my father's hired man, told us we could make one from two tin cans by tieing a string to their bottoms.

So we did. Believe it or not, it worked. At least we thought it did. There we'd be in the living room, hiding behind chairs, one of us hollerin' into a stupid tin can, while the other listened, a can cupped to his ear. Of course, we could hear! You could hear us all the way out to the milkhouse!

My grandparents did have a real phone, however. One of those beautiful oakwood kind that hung on the wall in the kitchen. Today, they're antiques. At its top were two circular metal bells. below those was a mouthpiece that stuck out into which one talked. On the side was a receiver on a long cord and a little crank.

Ah, yes! That was some kind of a telephone! Everybody was on a party line. Everybody had their own "ring," say two longs and a short, which you activated by twisting the little crank. And of course, none of those oldtimers believed the phone could carry a normal voice. So everybody hollered into the mouthpiece.

"Hello! Hello! Is that you Fred?" (Pause) "Dang it! Got cut off!" (More twists of the crank.) "Hello! Hello! Is that you, Fred?"

And the 'rubbering'. Let a neighbor's ring sound, and the temptation to eavesdrop was strong. Place a hand over the mouthpiece, slowly lift the receiver, and get the latest in neighborhood gossip. No one's life was private.

My Aunt Margaret had the first classy phone I remember. She and my Uncle Herb lived in town in kind of a spiffy neighborhood. And they had a private line!

In a corner of the living room on her desk, Aunt Margaret had one of those early model upright phones. Black, with a neat little mouthpiece and a receiver hanging next to it. But most important, it had a circular dial that made clicking noises when you made a call. I can still remember her number, 2-2718. That was before the days of area codes, of course.

And long distance calls! They were something else. Say I wanted to call a certain young lady to tell her that I had a weekend pass from the air base. Well, to the nearest pay phone I'd go. Drop in a nickel. Clink! And the operator would answer. "That will be 85 cents please!" she'd say. And into the slots at the top of the phone, I'd drop my coins, listening to them clink and clunk.

Today I punch in a number from a piece of plastic in my wallet, and the phone company sends me a bill at the end of the month.

It'll take me awhile to get used to my new toy. The instruction manual is filled with gobblety-gook. It'll take this old coot a little while to figure it all out.

In the meantime, don't call me...I'll call you!

April, 1994

# Inside The Rummage Sale Industry

Well, folks, each year at this time I know you anxiously await my annual report to you on the state of affairs in the rummage sale industry.

Being somewhat of a public-spirited citizen I feel it's my public duty to keep you informed on what's going on behind the scenes in this vast, complex, dynamic segment of our nation's economy.

The other day, I had a rare opportunity. I was granted an interview with the Chief Executive Officer, a real insider, by the way; of a major firm, Momma's Rummage Rooters LTD. This CEO, however, wishes to remain anonymous for obvious trade secret reasons. Please bear with her.

Momma's specializes in hard-to-find "rejectibles." Let's say, you need a water jug for your husband when he's out shearing Christmas trees in the hot summer sun. But you need one that has a lid that leaks, so he can cool both the inside and the outside of his belly at the same time. Momma's can find it for you.

Let's say he needs an air mattress to sleep on while he's off camping, fishing for walleyes. But you need one that will blow a patch in the middle of the night. Momma's can come through.

And you've got a two-year-old grandson that wants a blue toy automobile to scoot around on the driveway in. But its gotta have one flat tire. Call on Momma's!

Get the idea?

I asked the Chief Executive Officer some confidential questions -- to probe into the deepest workings of the industry. In short, what's feeding the bull dog? Here's what she told me.

1. WHAT ARE THE CURRENT GROWTH TRENDS IN YOUR RUMMAGE ROOTERS BUSINESS?

"We've had our usual excellent year. Sale volume is up. The market was very active this summer. There's always a new crop of grandmothers coming along looking for Christmas stockings for their grandkids. And new mothers that need potty chairs. All in all, we did well. Our financial losses were at a record high."

2. THERE'S TALK OF INFLATION AND A RECESSION, IF THAT HAPPENS, WILL THE RUMMAGE SALE INDUSTRY BE HURT?

"No, we'd gain from it. We'd dig a little deeper and sell at lower prices. You see, in this business the objective is to lose money, not make it. That takes special managerial talent."

3. THE RUMMAGE SALE INDUSTRY SEEMS TO BE DOMINATED BY FEMALE ENTREPRENEURS. IS THE GOVERNMENT THREATENING TO IMPOSE AFFIRMATIVE ACTION QUOTAS ON YOU TO PROVIDE MORE OPPORTUNITIES FOR MALES?

"It's the males' own fault! If they'd be willing to part with their junk like the females do, there'd be no problem. There's a market out there. We'd welcome the competition. We see men coming in all the time for worn-out monkey wrenches. And we can't keep old fishing rods in stock!"

4. ENVIRONMENTALISTS ARE PUSHING HARD

FOR MANDATORY RECYCLING OF OUR SOLID WASTE. IF THIS COMES TO PASS, WILL YOUR SUPPLY OF GOODS BE CUT OFF?

"No way! Our supply of solid waste is very solid. In fact, we resent the government sticking its nose into our industry. We invented recycling, as you well know. If the government was smart, it'd invite some of us rummage experts to Washington and use our expertise. We'd solve the problem in a hurry!"

5. SIGNS ADVERTISING RUMMAGE SALES VARY FROM CARDBOARD BOXES AND OLD PIECES OF PLYWOOD TO FANCY PRINTED JOBS. DO YOU FEEL LAWS SHOULD BE PASSED TO SET UNIFORM SIGN STANDARDS?

"Absolutely not! It would kill the creativity and destroy the uniqueness of our industry. It takes imagination to design good rummage sale signs. For example, you gotta use big balloons. The small ones deflate too fast. And you gotta get a lot of them, because the kids start to cry for a balloon. And you end up giving most of them away."

6. WITH THE MIDEAST CRISIS, GAS PRICES HAVE SKYROCKETED. HAVE SALES BEEN AFFECTED?

"Well, so far no. But I've noticed that there's more car pooling going on. There's even a taxi that comes full every week. I've been considering buying an old school bus to provide a shuttle service. I may be forced into that."

7. YOUR BUSINESS IS VERY SEASONAL. ARE YOU THINKING ABOUT DIVERSIFYING YOUR FAR-FLUNG EMPIRE INTO A YEAR-ROUND OPERATION?

"No, for several reasons. We're satisfied because we're losing enough money to keep us happy. Besides, there's only enough room in the house to store a half-year's inventory.

And we need the wintertime to dream and plan for the next season."

There you have it, folks! Exclusive, highly-classified insight, right from the mouth of a leading tycoon of a rummage sale conglomerate!

Anyone for a water jug?

October, 1990

# A Little On The Shy Side

Move over, world! Step aside a bit. Make a little room. Charlie Cool is coming on.

Who's Charlie Cool? Well, those of you who have been followers of the adventures of this column will recall that Charlie's my grandson. His antics have been reported here on several occasions in recent years; along with those of his little brother, Mighty Cool.

Charlie Cool isn't his real name of course, just a nickname I gave to him shortly after his birth, when he began to display certain personality attributes that qualified him for the tag. Grandpas, I've always believed, have the inalienable right to nickname their grandkids, you see!

Anyway, Charlie's growing up. It's showing in a lot of ways. Like how he's determined that he's now old enough to pick out his clothes for the day and to dress himself, proud of the fact that he's mastered the art of buttoning a shirt.

And it shows in the way he rides his two-wheeler bike down the driveway, scaring the bejeebers out of Grandma and me, as he whistles by, his flaming red hair flowing in the breeze, an excited smile creasing his dimpled face. I close my eyes as he does his fast turns around the parked pickup, fearing the training wheels will collapse, sending him crashing onto the blacktop. But Charlie's unphased.

You see it as he rides the backyard swing his dad made for

him. Faster, higher, he pumps until he's reached the absolute maximum speed and height the ropes will allow. And disappointed that he's reached that limit, wishing he could extend it further.

You hear it in the tale of his Easter morning. With the family getting ready for church, Charlie's mom dressed him out in his Sunday best outfit; white shirt, classy suspenders, trousers; and for the first time, a necktie. The necktie, that's what did it! All spiffied up, away Charlie went to check himself out in the mirror.

"Boy," he said, obviously pleased with what he saw, "I look just like a man!"

And, I hear it in our telephone conversations.

"Hey, Grandpa," he says, "I got a knock-knock joke for you!" Charlie's big on knock-knock jokes and riddles these days. "OK," I say. "Let's hear it."

"Knock-Knock," he comes back.

"Who's there?" I answer.

"Howie!"

"Howie who?"

"Howie doin' today!" he lays the punch line on me. And I can sense the mischievous smile in his voice.

Or the riddle he tested me with the other day.

"Why didn't the corn like the farmer?" he solemnly asked. "Gee, I really don't know," I answered, playing the game.

"Because he picked its ears!" he came back, punctuating the line with a hefty chuckle.

Yes, Charlie Cool's growing up. The signs are all around. And nowhere were they more obvious than the other day when his mom took him in to register for kindergarten. She admits to having some reservations as to how Charlie would handle it.

Arriving at the 'ELEMENTARY' school, as Charlie now proudly refers to the place, the two were greeted by the school personnel handling the registration. And Charlie was tactfully informed that he'd have to go into the adjoining room for some tests.

Well, that threw him a bit. But he handled it with his usual aplomb, taking the lady's hand; and in his best polite manner, telling her, "I'm a little shy, you know!"

Well, time passed, and mom nervously awaited his return, a bit apprehensive. Finally the door opened and out stepped Charlie, the lady, and the young man conducting the tests; all three wearing big smiles. All had gone well.

"See you in kindergarten next September, Kyle!" the lady called as Charlie and his mom prepared to leave.

"Yup, I'll see you then when I'm grown up," Charlie responded. And then an afterthought. "Yup, I'll see you when I'm five!"

Move over a trifle, kindergarten!

May, 1991

# Where The Blueberries Grow

*"...I still know where the blueberries grow... there's a winding stream off an old sand road..."*

The words are from a beautiful new song by Pete and Dorothy Lund on their Pinery Road label. The Lunds, from Eagle River, write folk music about northern Wisconsin's rich cultural past.

And blueberries are what this column today is all about.

I spent a day recently with Guy Johnson. Johnson grew up in the Webb Lake area northwest of Spooner. He's now 94 years young, and he's been a berry picker all his life. Not only blueberries, but raspberries and strawberries too. Five trips he made in recent weeks to Phil Lindeman's berry ranch west of Shell Lake to pick strawberries, berries that he gave away to his many friends.

But blueberries, wild ones that is, are his first love. And rightly so, because as a young boy growing up on his folks' farm in northern Burnett County, he had plenty of occasion to pick the fruit. "I remember times when the bushes would be just blue," he told me.

But first a few words about Johnson himself.

"I was born in Eau Claire," he said. "My folks brought me to Spooner in 1901, when I was six months old. My dad had a horse and two cows when he settled near Webb Lake to farm that sand. He took a job working on the railroad in Spooner during the week, and he'd walk the 24 miles back and forth on weekends. Just trails through the woods back then."

Johnson remembers trips to Spooner by horse and wagon. "Stop here," he said, as I drove a country road. "You see that big white pine over there. That's where my dad would stop to rest and feed the horses."

And he remembers the big forest fires that raged across the country. "Dad built all of our buildings out of logs from pine trees killed by the Hinckley fire, the house, the barn, and the chicken coop."

Thus he talked, and I listened, as we wound our way through his old familiar haunts. Past the site of the first schoolhouse in the township, to which his two older brothers walked four miles to attend. And a visit to the shore of Webb Lake where a resort he owned once stood. Over Webb Creek, where he watched pine logs being driven downstream to the Namekagon River, logs that eventually were floated into the St. Croix and on to sawmills at Stillwater, Minnesota.

And finally to the Namekagon barrons country, where his blueberry memories are the strongest. "There used to be an Indian settlement here," he said, sweeping his hand across the jack pine and aspen forest as we walked. "About a dozen log houses. Here's where John Kanabec lived, their leader. That hole in the ground was his well. Over there is a burial ground." And together we gazed at the sunken depressions where graves existed.

"In July and August the Indian people would come here by horse and wagon to camp and pick blueberries," he explained. "I'd come here twice a week to buy their berries.

*Guy Johnson remembers when blueberries were harvested with rakes.*

A crate holding 16 quarts was worth around a dollar. I bought from Otis Taylor, the Bearhearts, Jay Staples, Guss Cadott, John Holmes, Sam Blackburn, and others."

Johnson re-sold the berries to a buyer named Munstad. "He bought berries all over the area," Guy said. "I saw his wagon so loaded it took a four-horse team to pull it. The crates would be piled 8 to 10 high. The berries were then shipped to the big cities."

In those early days, a device called a 'blueberry rake' was sometimes used to harvest the berries, Johnson said. "Charley and George Christner, friends of my dad, once picked 16 crates in one day with rakes. But the rakes stripped the vines, and the berries were more mushy, and didn't keep as well. Eventually, the rakes were outlawed."

On we slowly travelled, over a trail barely passable for my truck. At its end, on the edge of a large bog, we stopped.

"This is the Kanabec Swamp," Guy said, as we walked into the hummocks of leatherleaf. And there we found blueberries, clusters of ripe fruit, hanging like blue pearls from their vines.

"We could get enough for a couple pies here!" I called. "Yeah, but they're on the small side. The best spot is over there," Guy answered, pointing across the swamp.

But we'd come that day to talk about berries, not to pick them. That would wait for another time.

"Guy," I said, as we headed home, "What is there about picking berries that you like so much?"

"I don't really know," he replied. "There's something about it. I just like to pick them!"

And his words brought me back to Pete and Dorothy Lund's blueberry song.

*"...We need some things to count on, you see. The spruce bogs in blossom and labarador tea. The red-breasted grossbeaks, the return of the crows..."*

*"...From out of my past comes an answer I know..."*

*"...And I know where the blueberries grow..."*

July, 1995

# Listen Up, Miz Spring!

He-e-y... Miz Spri-i-ing!!

Can you hear me? I know you're out there! I've been watching some of your workings lately !

Like my driveway, for instance. I found it the other day. It's been missing, you know. Since last Halloween when that character, "Wimp" Fall, allowed it to be buried under two feet of snow.

Oh, I knew it was around someplace, somewhere between the street and the garage door. And sure enough, the other day, after you'd sent some of your warm rays, there it was!

Same with my roof! Oh, I figured it had to be somewhere between the back porch and the chimney. But then, I couldn't be sure. Until you came along, that is. It finally showed up, neat brown shingles and all, just where it'd been left last October. Before old Wimp let it get lost, of course.

And my lawn! The jury's still out on that. It's probably where I left it. But then, who really knows? Since Wimp let things go to pot on Trick or Treat night, I've barely been able to see over the tops of the snowbanks.

I'm optimistic, though. I say that because, on the path to Butch, my fearless huntin' and fishin' dog's house, where I've been running the snowblower going on five months now, you'd exposed a little patch of brown dead-grass-covered sod.

Ah, but it's beautiful -- a sight for winter-sore eyes! Every day, the little plot has grown a tad larger. And when my feet touch it, as I walk to fetch Butch, I rejoice!

Then the other night, as I took Momma out for a bite to eat, there in the road laid a dead skunk. Skunks hibernate. And there was one that obviously had declared winter officially over; yet it'd been 'terminated' on the poor critter's first night out on the town, flattened probably by a careening '84 Toyota four-by-four! Still, it's death there in the middle of the road, represented an indisputable signal of spring.

And the geese! There they were that late afternoon, as I returned from an ice fishing trip. Six fat Canadian honkers, stretched out in a line, silhouetted against the sky, flapping their wings in unison. Were they beautiful!

Even the plant world is beginning to stir. I was refilling a bird feeder the other day, the one next to the dining room window where the chickadees and redpolls flit just on the other side of the glass; where Butch sat for hours this winter studying the squirrels while they feasted on sunflower seeds within inches of his nostrils. And there, next to the foundation of the house, curling up from the warmed soil, were yellow-green shoots... sprouts of young sunflower seedlings, freshly germinating from seeds the birds and squirrels had dropped.

And soon, the maple syrup folks will be busy tapping their trees and hanging their buckets.

I say that because recently I strapped on the snowshoes and hiked back into my tree farm woods. There, standing a naked-yellow, were two sugar maple saplings, their bark chewed off by hungry grey squirrels seeking the sweet cambium innerwood. And seeping from the wounds, were the first drippings of maple sap.

And Bernice Abrahamzon reported just a week or so ago that she'd picked a bouquet of pussy willows. What surer sign of spring is there, than willow buds bursting into furry bloom.

Ah yes, Miz Spring, I do believe you're out there.

What better evidence could I have than the two young mothers happily wheeling their baby carriages down the street the other day. You know, the kind that remind me of a convertible car, because their plastic tops fold down.

There they were, two young moms, smiling, conversing busily with each other, out giving their newborns a breath of your balmy air. A beautiful sight... a sure sign that you've got Old Man Winter on the ropes.

Keep it up! Keep those soft breezes blowing! We're cheering you on, eager to embrace you.

Just remember one thing. Take a lesson from Wimp Fall, that jerk that let us down last Halloween!

Easter's coming.,

No snow in the kids' Easter baskets, please!

March, 1992

# Air Travel

"What airline, ma'am?" the driver asks, loading our bags into his shuttle bus at the motel.

"USAir," Momma answers. She and I are about to catch a flight from the Minneapolis airport headed for North Carolina, for a week of lolly-gaggin', as they say down south, with daughter and her family. It's a little after six in the morning, and though there's major road construction, traffic is almost non-existent. Our driver makes good time to the airport.

At USAir, two sidewalk ticket clerks stand ready to check our luggage through. Momma's prepared, tickets in hand. our seats have been assigned. All we need are our boarding passes. The clerk fingers through the envelope Momma hands him. "Jacksonville, North Carolina," he says, and begins to attach tags to our bags.

I turn to Momma and say, jokingly, "Just so they don't go to Jacksonville, Florida!" The clerk stops, gasps. I look over at what he'd been doing, and sure as heck -- our bags are tagged for Jacksonville, FLORIDA!

"I'm sorry, sir!" he apologizes. "I made a mistake. I'm glad you caught it." And he rips away the errant tags. A close call.

"Gate 32 on the Blue Concourse," he adds. And we make our way through the nearly empty terminal. Saturday mornings are a good time to fly, I decide.

A brief wait, and we board. Our seats are in the tail section, near the "kitchen", and I'm getting hungry. We're scheduled for a breakfast somewhere between Minneapolis and Pittsburgh, our one stop enroute to Charlotte where we'll change planes.

I snap my seat belt, settle in, and pick up a brochure that describes the plane. We'll be flying on a MD 80 it says. MD stands for MacDonald Douglas. It carries 135, and all seats are full. Jet engines begin to whine, and we creep toward the runway. A short pause; the plane inches forward, big engines roar, and we lift into the clear early morning sky.

"This is your captain," the intercom announces. "Welcome aboard Flight 347 bound for Pittsburgh and Charlotte. We'll be flying at 33,000 feet. It's going to be a little bumpy over Lake Michigan, so the seat belt sign will remain on."

Just my luck, I think. That's when I'll be drinking my coffee!

A stewardess, tall and blond with a face like Vanna White's, bends over us. "The egg omelet or pancake breakfast?" she asks. One of each, we tell her.

Momma is already visiting with the lady in the seat next to her. The lady's a missionary, originally from Grantsburg, now living in Hong Kong. I ask how things are in mainland China, and she wiggles her fingers, a signal that I interpret to mean touchy and tenuous.

"We didn't spill," Momma laughs, as Vanna picks up our breakfast trays, dropping styrofoam cups into a big white plastic bag with "USAir" on its side. "I'd like one of those for my rummage sale-ing," Momma pleads. The stewardess smiles and on her next trip, drops one off.

Touchdown at Pittsburgh. A 45 minute layover... and on to Charlotte.

The passenger scene changes. A young family of four moves along the center aisle. The boy, about five, carries a stuffed baseball player with "Pittsburgh Pirates" across its shirt. The little girl asks her mother if her doll can have a seat. Overhead compartments snap and bang as carry-on luggage is stowed. The hour flight to Charlotte is smooth as silk.

But we get in ten minutes late. And our connection to Jacksonville is tight, 25 minutes as scheduled, which leaves us fifteen to make the quarter mile hike through the concourse. We arrive at the gate just as Flight 1435 is called to board.

"Well, we're on our final leg," I half-whisper to Momma, as we take our seats. The B727-200 has only half its seats filled. United States Marines dressed in civilian garb, yet apparent by their sun-tanned faces, close-cropped haircuts, and muscular physiques, make up a good share. Two Marine bases, Camp Lejeune and the New River Air Station, are located at Jacksonville.

"Would you like something to drink?" a friendly stewardess asks. I take a can of Sprite, Momma a cup of coffee. All goes well 'till we hit an air pocket, dumping brown liquid on her pink blouse. "Well, you almost made it!" I chide her.

Eagerly, we step along the tunnel-like ramp toward the terminal. There, familiar faces, daughter and her family stand ready to greet us.

We're in North Carolina -- for some lolly-gaggin'!

August, 1990

# Christmas Vacations

"Christmas vacation," we always called this time of year as kids, back in my school days, when we'd get a week or so off from our studies about now. And Christmas vacation, it's still called today.

For some reason this year, I find myself looking back to those old days. I really can't say why. Maybe it's the easy winter we've experienced so far, the mild days and the light snow on the ground. Somehow, I'm reminded of similar times when Christmas vacations meant a brief freedom from books and desks, a chance to have some fun in the outdoors, to do boy stuff.

A lot of good memories come back.

Like the very first I recall, Christmas breaks as a youngster in my early grades, when I was six, seven, eight years old. Out to my grandfolks' farm I'd be sent, to spend some time, to get better acquainted with granddad, grandmother and a bevy of aunts and uncles.

Late December was wood-making time for grandpa. And there in his woodlot I got my first taste of timber and logging. There, in the company of my uncles, I learned to swing an axe, to pull a crosscut saw, and to drive a wedge; skills and feelings for trees that stayed with me all of my life.

There'd be some hunting. What a thrill I'd know as I trailed along behind my Uncle Amy, the best outdoorsman in the family and a very good man with a shotgun and rifle, as he poked along brushy fence rows, to kick out a cottontail rabbit or two. Dressed out, the critters would be hung to freeze on the back porch. And when my vacation was over, and I left for home, proudly I carried them along.

As the years passed and I grew older and more independent, Christmas vacations began to take on a different meaning. A cluster of friends gradually formed, neighborhood buddies, youngsters of ten, twelve years of age.

Christmas vacation usually meant snow on the ground. And over at Deak's Hill, the gang of us would gather, to belly-flop our sleds down its steep slope, the runners of our American Flyers hissing and the wind created by our breakneck speed whistling in our ears.

Or to the little pond in Newman's woods, where with scoop shovels borrowed from our fathers' graneries, we'd clear the ice's surface. Then we'd sit on stumps or fallen trees to fasten our old-fashioned "clamp" skates to the soles of our shoes. Or, if you were one of the more fortunates, lace on a pair of brand-new "shoe" skates, a recent Christmas gift perhaps.

Hockey sticks would be contrived from crooked saplings, pucks of knotty chunks of wood. And for hours, we'd skate; slipping, sliding, tripping, falling, amid shouts of laughter and boisterous bravado.

Boyhood years passed into teenage years, however. And the play went out of Christmas vacation. On two sides of the world, a war raged. Life took on a deadly serious side, as one by one, I watched friends leave, several of whom I never saw again.

And ultimately a call of my own. I've never forgotten, as an eighteen-year-old, that furlough in 1945. Ahead an overseas assignment awaited... and that Christmas vacation became one of goodbyes.

Christmas vacations were never the same after that. Gone were boyhood interests, replaced with adult pursuits. Like the hitchhiking home from college in 1949 to slip a ring on the finger of a demure young lady with auburn bangs hanging down over her forehead; a ring she's worn ever since, for the more than forty-two years she's been at my side.

Christmas vacations have since been times of kids of our own, of them excitedly opening presents from under brightly-lighted trees, of winter travels together to visit and bond with their grandparents over checkerboards and jigsaw puzzles.

And in time, to watch as they too have moved out into the world, creating families of their own, and grandkids that bring joy to these Christmas vacations today.

Life, as Christmas vacations goes on. And we're grateful.

December, 1992

# Lady Summer's Farewell

That grand old dame, Lady Summer, bid me adieu the other day, slipping away quietly, without fanfare, much like the way she arrived last June.

I should have known she had leaving on her mind when the furnace kicked on one late-August night... and I had to get up to shut the windows. And I should have noticed a morning or two later when the yellow school buses arrived, convoy-style, at the high school down at the corner; as a loose parade of youngsters traipsed along our street, backpacks slung over their shoulders.

Then, I should have sensed the Lady's plans, that she was packing her bags, as I watched farmers maneuver their green-and-yellow combines across their oats fields, spewing trails of golden straw behind them. Again, I should have guessed when I stopped at the pickup trucks of roadside vendors for bags of sweet corn, and paused to admire boxes of green peppers, red tomatos, and purple new potatoes, fresh from the fields.

And I should have realized that she was about to hit the road as I plucked a pail of blackberries along a country roadside, amidst the blooms of brown-eyed susans and daisies, while a horde of bees filled the air with their buzzing, as they frenetically gathered nectar for their winter stores.

I should have recognized those signs. I should have read

from them that another summer was winding down. But I didn't.

It didn't really hit me that the Lady was waving goodbye until an afternoon or two later... as I was dumping my boat into Shell Lake for a try at the walleyes. There, at the edge of the boat landing, stood a clump of sumac, its leaves beginning to turn a crimson red. Only then did it really dawn on me that summer was gone.

I pushed off and began my casting, and more unmistakable signals. The lake was strangely quiet. Only a week or two earlier it'd been alive with powerboats and water skiers. Now I'd be alone, the only boat afloat. Overhead a half-dozen mallards wheeled; full-bodied, strong-winged birds, letting it be known that they too would soon respond to an ancient instinctive migratory urge, and leave.

The early evening air too told me that a change had taken place, that things were different. The sun disappeared behind the wooded hills to the west. As it did, I felt the bite of the night air, a chill borne on a breeze that seeped inside my collar, prompting me to cover my head with my parka's hood.

Lady Summer was on her way, no doubt about it.

And I saw more evidence of her departure on a trout stream recently.

A trout stream in the spring and early summer is a thing of magnificent beauty as it throbs with vitality. The water is fresh and cold and flows with power and energy. Along its banks life flourishes; flowers, birds and animals that fill the air with scent and sound and sights.

But wade the same water in late summer or fall, and the scene changes. Green waterweeds slow the stream's muscle, and the bankside vegetation's lush green is replaced with the drabness of dying foliage. The air, once filled with bird song

*Summer ended with a catch of trout.*

and fluttering wings, becomes noticeably silent.

That's how I found my trout stream the other day. The stream, once vibrant with activity, was preparing to rest. Its cycle of life and reproduction was over for another year, as nature intended it to be.

Yes, I caught some fish, mostly brook trout, resplendent

in their fall colors of brilliant blue-black, orange and violet. And along the banks, amongst the lavender heads of milkweeds, floated orange monarch butterflies. Through the alders, occasional pairs of black and yellow goldfinches flitted. Tracks in the mud told of critters now moving more furtively at night.

But a season had passed. That was obvious.

Lady Summer had said her farewell.

September, 1993

# Playing Cards

Ah, yes! Taking-it-easy time is here! January and February! The dead of winter! When I look forward to "crashing."

Finished for the year are the tree farm projects of the past summer and fall. Gone is the hustle and bustle of the holidays. And now I'm ready to settle in for a long winter's nap, so to speak. Like an old boar bear, I'm ready to go into hibernation.

Well, not really. That's a bit of an overstatement, to be sure. There'll be plenty to do. Some ice fishing, some reading. January-February is the only time I pick up a book, for instance. It's then, when the nights are long and the snowbanks stand tall outside the window, that I truly enjoy curling up with a good book.

I expect there'll be some socializing, visits long overdue by Momma and me to friends. We northerners, those of us who stick around over winter, that is, know the pleasure of sitting around on a night when the north wind is whistling, to just plain visit.

And as I find myself looking forward to some of that, thoughts come floating back from times before television... thoughts about what folks did for winter relaxation and recreation. Memories come to mind about card games.

"Playing cards," all my relatives called those pastimes.

Everybody I knew, it seemed, played cards. Today, it's pretty much a dying art. Sure, there are still ladies' bridge clubs. And I suppose, there are a few back rooms of small-town taverns where old-timers still gather for a hand or two of "shmear". But I can't remember the last time I heard of someone holding a "card party."

Card parties were big in my boyhood. In country school basements, in church halls. Folks came from all around to play... and socialize. All for modest little prizes and a piece of homemade cake and a cup of coffee.

And how can I forget the Sunday afternoons when kinfolks would gather in my grandparents' kitchens for a few games of euchre before the cows had to be milked. The walls would echo with whoops and hollers! The old wooden kitchen tables would resound with the banging of knuckles and pounding of fists!

Talk about competition! Let a partner misplay a trump card, causing a hand to be lost, and a lifetime relationship would be threatened. And never be it said, that a little underhanded play didn't occur. Oh, no pure out-and-out cheating. Just signals passed with winks of eyes and bumps of feet under the table.

Then, to invite another couple over to play cards on a Saturday evening was common. Plunk the baby on a bed to sleep amidst the coats; set up the table (a sign of affluence was to own a card table); pull up a floor lamp for light; turn on the radio, maybe to WLS out of Chicago with its Barn Dance Show, and you'd be ready for some rousing 500.

A standard rule was that husband and wife were never to be partners; the reasoning being, it seemed, that there was less potential for criticism of your partner's play. After all, it's a little hard to tell your best friend's wife that she bid too high, especially in the presence of your best friend. Card games can get very serious at times. So the system tended to keep things on an even keel. At least most of the time.

The first card game I personally played was with one of my grandfathers. I was still in grade school when he taught me a game called "66." I've long forgotten how it's played. Except that two people could play, and the cards had point values. At the end of each hand, points were added. I learned more about arithmetic playing 66 with my grandpa, than I did in school!

And cribbage, the one game that I still understand, I learned to play from my Uncle Herb and Aunt Margaret. They'd sit for hours in evenings listening to the Fibber McGee or Amos 'n Andy shows, while they played cribbage.

They were very good players. One of the nice things about the game is that two, three, or four people can play. So I'd join them as they taught me the fine points, impressed with how fast they could count their hands. And listening several times to the story of how Aunt Margaret had once held a perfect 29 hand. And how Uncle Herb had called the local newspaper to report her achievement, making her a celebrity for a week or so!

Playing cards filled a big niche in our social order of those times. Those old-timers were certainly not couch potatoes.

Who knows? I might just break out a deck and the cribbage board one of these nights.

That's if I can stay awake, of course.

January, 1995

# Li'l Red

My backyard, over the years, has become sort of a sanctuary for orphan trees. Without really trying, I've allowed it to become kind of a home for tree waifs that, for one reason or another, have needed a helping hand.

There's a little tree growing back by the dog kennel these days. It's a red maple. Technically, its name is Acer rubrum. But I've come to call the little seedling "Li'l Red." Which implies that it's a boy tree. Which may or may not be true.

Now, one more tree in my life is no big deal. Having been around the forestry game for more than forty years, I've had a very satisfying association with trees. Our 160-acre Tree Farm alone, where I spend a lot of my time, probably has a couple million trees on it, if one counts all the little squirts that poke their noses out of the ground each spring. Most of which don't survive because of the rigors they face in a harsh environment.

Trees have been the object of a lot of affection in my life. Starting way back, when as a youngster I'd trudge in the snow behind my uncles to my grandfather's woodlot where, with crosscut saws and axes, oaks and hickories would be felled. Trees that later would be made into lumber for stanchions in the cow barn, fence posts to keep the young stock out of the corn, and firewood to heat the big brick farmhouse where grandpa and his family lived.

So it's natural for me to have a warm spot in my heart for my backyard trees. I walk among them, some I've planted, others that Mother Nature did, and I look them over critically, and help them along if I can.

Such is the case with Li'l Red. He's become a special tree to me, special because he's got courage, guts if you will, as trees go.

He's, as best I can figure, three years old now. I noticed him first a couple summers ago, just a pair of tri-lobed leaves poking from a tiny stem. Where he was growing, however, made him different. And therein lies a larger story, one about life and death in the tree community.

Li'l Red grows in a crevice next to a rotting stump. The stump is all that remains of a three-foot thick elm tree that once stood there. A majestic tree, standing so tall, that by summer mid-afternoons the sun, though still high in the sky, would be shielded, and our house would be bathed in cool comforting shade.

But then came the Dutch Elm disease. I feared that might happen. And I even bought a fungicide and a kit to inject the tree each spring. That helped, and for awhile I was optimistic that I'd save the big elm. But in time the deadly virus won out, and the tree had to come down.

Its stump has remained, however. There on its top, the half of a whiskey barrel has rested for ten years or so. Filled with dirt, each spring Momma plants her barrel flower pot with impatiens and begonias. Their colorful blooms brighten the back yard all summer long.

As time has passed though, the old stump has begun to rot. And there, in the decaying wood, protected from the lawn mower, Li'l Red has taken up residence. He's shown considerable vigor since his modest birth two summers ago.

Last year, he grew about a foot-and-a-half. And I was pleased to see this past spring that Thumper, our resident cottontail rabbit, chose to not nip Red's tender tip for a winter snack.

But this year, Li'l Red really sprouted. Apparently, he's got his root system firmly established and finds the nutrients being released by the rotting stump to his liking. Because he's shot up almost four feet. He's big enough to swish my leg as I cut the grass, and he's taken on an identity, standing out green against Butch's kennel.

He's a fine stripling of a sapling as he waves in the breeze above Momma's red flowers and the crumbling elm stump, exuding life and vitality once again to a plot of ground where a noble tree once grew.

He joins the five-foot balsam fir that popped up where a balsam has no right to be growing. And the two white ashes that John Borkenhagen gave me at one of his Hayward State Nursery open houses. And the Norway pine that came from a Logging Congress. And the two mountain ashes that I transplanted after they sprouted under the big burr oak out front.

Twiggy tots like Li'l Red can sure make running a tree orphanage fun.

August, 1994

# Odyssey Of The Odd Couple

It's an improbable, implausible tale, one that tugs at the heart. It's a story about a unique friendship, that of a cow for a dog... and vice versa.

Scottie Hergert told it to me recently. "The Odyssey of the Odd Couple," he calls the tale.

Back in 1986, Hergert was living on the farm his grand-parents homesteaded many years ago three miles southeast of Barronett. "In June that year, a farmer gave me a bull calf. At the time, bull calves weren't worth the gas to haul them to market," he began.

A Black Angus-Jersey cross, the animal was a dark black-brown in color. And being only three days old, it had to be bottle-fed. "Critter," he named the calf.

"Well," Scottie continued, "at the same time, I had a four-month-old black Labrador pup called 'Pepper'. And every time I'd feed Critter his bottle, Pepper would be there to lick any spilled milk from his face. I really think the calf got to believe the dog was its mother!"

And thus, the strong bond of affection grew between them; becoming inseparable, sharing the barn together, sleeping side by side. "They had their own little straw pile," Scottie recalls."If Critter was in his pen, Pepper would usually be there beside him."

Months passed and Critter grew into steerhood. With that

maturity, came a hatred for confinement, perhaps because his pal enjoyed freedom he didn't. "A couple of times, Critter butted out the siding of the old barn and got loose," Hergert said. "But all I had to do to find the steer was to look for Pepper."

"One day Critter followed Pepper over to a neighbor's pond when the dog went to check on some wild ducks. The only way I could get the steer home was to drive down the road with Pepper walking alongside the car. Then Critter would follow."

The two even shared their food. "The steer would eat the dog's food, and the dog would eat the steer's food," Hergert said.

Then, on a snowy winter day in January, the two bosom buddies decided to see the world, to run away from home.

"Critter broke out of the barn that day," Hergert tells. "When I came home in late afternoon, I found where the two had wandered around the yard for awhile, then headed northwest."

Driving into Barronett, Scottie began to ask if anyone had seen the pair. "Before I'd get the words out of my mouth, people would say 'You mean the odd couple? Yeah, they wandered around town for an hour'."

Scottie searched all that evening, checking with neighbors, but except in Barronett, no one had seen the pair.

"The next morning I got up early. A blizzard was blowing. You couldn't track anything," he said. "After searching all day, I decided to call the Rice Lake and Shell Lake radio stations. I put 'em on the radio: Lost, one black lab and one steer!"

Because he had no phone on his farm, Hergert used his cousin Luke's phone number. And the next morning, Luke got a call from a farmer asking if he was "the party looking for the odd couple." The temperature outside was 25 below zero.

Well, Scottie and Luke drove to the farmer's home, some eight miles away. There they found Critter and Peppers' tracks. "They'd have come in the house, if I'd have opened the door," the farmer told them.

"You could see where the steer had helped himself to some corn in the crib," Scottie said. And two miles down the road, the snow was packed down where Pepper had feasted on a deer skeleton that had been discarded in the ditch.

"Nearby was a logging road with a gate. You could see tracks where Pepper had led Critter around it," Hergert said. "Luke and I got out and started tracking on foot. We got back in the woods about a half a mile, and there they stood, both of them, looking at us like what are you guys doin' here?"

"We had a rope which we tied to the steer. But Critter wouldn't budge unless Pepper led the way," Hergert told.

Thus, ended the Odyssey of the Odd Couple. The two wanderers were returned to Hergert's farm.

"Both were fine, not even hungry," he added. "Of course, I had to patch up the old barn again."

Today, Critter's gone. But, Pepper, the other half of the Odd Couple, remains Hergert's faithful companion.

August, 1991

# And "Hah" To You, Miz Spring!

That famously fickle female, Miz Spring, came waltzing through the backyard the other day. Right on cue, as a matter of fact. On March 20, her opening day; so the calendar says.

There she was pirouetting petitely, like a ballerina; her gossamer gown flowing in the breeze, a happy smile caressing her lips, a blissful glow shining in her eyes, blowing kisses softly across the landscape.

Ah, but she looked beautiful prancing about the puddles. Surely, she was for real, I thought. Surely, Old Man Winter was in full retreat, kicked unceremoniously out of town by this fair damsel.

Hah!

This morning I awoke to six inches of snow on the driveway. And as I write, I'm recuperating from a round of fun and games with the snowblower, the machine that I'd gazed so wistfully at the day Miz Spring had danced down the driveway. For a moment, I'd considered tucking that wondrous device away for the season.

Hah!

How dumb can a guy get? So we've had a great March, one that came in like a lamb and looked like it would go out like one too. Warm, sunny days that melted the ice on the street out front, sending rivlets of water gushing down the gutters. Weather that brought back memories of my boyhood, when grandfather and a neighbor would huddle by the barn door. "Yup! Sure looks like we're gonna have an early spring," they'd say.

Hah!

I even got carried away by that first warm rain. There I was, out at the tree farm, kicking off my spring work agenda. Boy, it felt good as I moved along the rows of spruce, giving the little buggers a haircut with my long-handled shearing knife. Chop! Chop! Slash! Slash! The green twigs flew as I shaped my charges into Christmas trees.

Oh sure, underfoot small patches of snow lingered, escapees from Miz Spring's warm sunshine. But in between, my boots squished in the soft mud of freshly-warmed soil. Ah, how wonderful, that first reunion with Mother Earth again.

And then the rain! Softly it fell, slowly at first, then bigger drops, closer together, enough to cause me to call it quits. But surely with it, the frost would go out, my road would dry, and I could soon get about my chores in earnest.

Hah!

I even got taken in by the backyard birds and animals. All through those thirty-below days of January and February, I'd faithfully kept the feeder filled with sunflower seeds for the chickadees and nuthatches. On two trees hung hefty chunks of suet for the woodpeckers to peck.

On an oak, hung the squirrel feeder Helen German had given me a couple years ago. Every morning I dutifully skewered a fresh ear of corn on its nail. And within minutes, those bushy-tailed moochers would be there feeding, kernels of corn dropping to the ground for Thumper, the cottontail rabbit that lived in our woodpile, to munch later in the moonlight.

But with Miz Spring's appearance, old Thump had moved on, back to the woods. And the squirrels and birds too. Surely that was a good sign, a good omen, that winter had departed.

Hah!

And the most irrefutable evidence of all... Momma's attitude. I can always tell when spring is near. She gets a mite excited. "I'm not ready for spring," she'll say. "I don't have all my winter projects done!"

This year was no different. Mid-March sent her scurrying into a closet for the boxes of old family photographs she'd vowed to frame and hang on the living room wall before the snowbanks disappeared.

Frantically, she worked, evidence that spring was almost upon us, that winter was certainly winding down.

Hah!

I should know better than to trust you, Miz Spring. Every year it's the same. Along you come with your old song-and-dance routine, sending my spirits rising, building my hopes with your sweet talk.

Here's what I have to say to that...

Hah!

April, 1994

# The Third Annual Last Rummage Sale

Well, it's over, folks! It's history! Another rummage sale, one appropriately called "The Third Annual Last Rummage Sale" is now fading, as all good things do, into the past.

Rummage sales, also known as garage and yard sales, are an American tradition. I don't know if folks in Tanzania, Tibet and Timbuktu hold rummage sales. But here in the good old USA, we sure do. They're a colorful cog in our culture.

And over the years, at our house, Momma has done her part. Oh, she's slowed down a bit, doesn't cover the Friday morning beat like she once did. But she still keeps her hand in the game, like the sale she conducted a past weekend.

Observer that I am, it's not easy watching the agony she goes through to get a sale off the ground, or should I say, onto a motley array of tables and racks in the garage.

"It takes months of thinking," she says. "The hard part is to find the energy and stamina. But you know it's time for a sale when you can't get into the closets anymore!"

It's then that my role moves from observer to hired hand. Clean the garage! Move out my beloved boat! Carry in the picnic table! Get the handy-dandy clothes racks I made down from the attic!

The final push comes, of course, the day before sale time. That's when I make what seems to be endless trips up the basement stairs carrying boxes and bags of "stuff"... goodies that are outgrown, outdated and outlandish.

Laid out meticulously on the garage tables, the items all have to be priced with little colored tape tags. Pricing, I found out, is a science. "That's the hardest part of a rummage sale," Momma says. "To decide what something's worth and what's fair."

And the advertising! A clever ad in the paper, and a sign down at the corner, usually embellished with colorful balloons. Balloons are big! Not this year. "I just didn't have oomph to blow them up!" she said.

And her helpers! There's a cadre of a half-dozen or so that join in, and the garage is alive with the sound of their voices, their laughter.

"Some brought a few things to sell, and then they stayed to help me. They're good salespeople and they're good company," Momma said. "I couldn't have done it without my friends!"

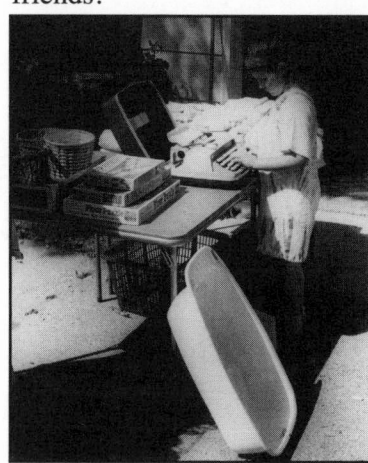

A young rummage sale shopper tests a typewriter.

So was the sale a success? Well, how could it fail?

"It was great," she says. "The weather was perfect. Not like a couple years when I held sales in the snow because I waited too long. It's not as much fun when you have to wear winter coats and boots!"

What were some of the high points, I asked.

"All the nice people that

came, especially the cute little kids. Like the little girl, about five, who said when her grandmother bought her a hat, 'Don't you have a mirror in here so I can see myself?' "

"And another, who was so excited when she found a pair of high-heel shoes she wanted, which her mother bought for her. Out to the car she tromped wearing them, leaving behind the sandals she'd been wearing."

I hung around the sale awhile myself, and I second what Momma says about the kids. Like the cute little girl I saw who bought a long string of blue beads for a quarter to match her blue-and-white dress and the blue bow in her hair. She was a proud little lady as she left.

And I spoke with Fred Mundt, who was looking for the steel box that holds a link-and-pin coupler from a narrow-gauge railway car or engine. Fred said the box is needed for the Spooner Railroad Museum.

I'd put my snowblower up for sale, and it was gone in no time. Started on the first pull, too. Momma said she could have sold a half-a-dozen. A sign of a bad winter coming? I hope not.

Men shop differently than women, Momma says. "When men come, they pick up what they want and they're on their way. I've never had a rummage sale yet where they haven't tried to buy the garden rakes and shovels and Bob's fishing rods, which aren't for sale!"

And so another exercise in American free enterprise is memory. Will it be Momma's final fling?

"When I had my first last sale, I thought it would be my last," she told me. "But I didn't stop accumulating stuff. So I don't know if this last last sale will be my last or not."

(Hope all you folks out there can follow that!)

August, 1996

# Truly A Miracle!

I'm doing just fine, thank you!

What's that all about, you say. Well, by chance maybe you've seen me running around lately wearing a pair of those fancy wrap-around, ala Hollywood-type, sunglasses. If so, pay no heed! I haven't lost it! I'm still my old 'Plain and Simple' self, believe me.

And I'm doing just fine, thank you... recovering from cataract surgery on my left eye, that is.

The story begins almost two years ago, as a doctor peered into my eyes with one of those little examining gadgets. "Hmmm!" he murmured. "Looks like you've got the start of a cataract here."

He was right, of course.

So at six-month intervals, I began seeing an ophthalmologist, having its progress checked. And with each succeeding examination, I found my vision deteriorating. At the beginning, yes, I could read some of the letters on his wall chart. But each time, that became a bit more difficult. Until in January, my last checkup, when I could read absolutely nothing.

And inside, I knew that surgery was imminent... if I wanted to retain my eyesight in that eye.

"I think it's time," my good doctor had said. "Think about it."

I did... overnight.

The decision wasn't easy. I had a 95 percent chance for success, my doctor had said. Surely, those are excellent odds. But what about the other five percent? With my luck, maybe that's where I'd fall. Then what?

Still, what choice do I have, I told myself. I can barely see with the eye now, and things are going to only get worse.

And in the morning, I called my doctor. "Schedule me for surgery as soon as possible," I told him. I wanted to get on with it, get it over.

Eye cataracts are a very common affliction, I've learned. An informational booklet put out by Storz Ophthalmics Inc., the firm that manufactured the artificial lens that's been implanted in my eye, helped greatly to ease my concerns. Each year more than one million surgeries are performed in the United States.

And what is a cataract? Well, in layman's language, the natural lens in the eye becomes clouded, turning opaque. As a result, light entering the eye is diffused and a blurred image results on the retina at the back of the eye.

While their cause remains unknown, cataracts are a part of the normal aging process, affecting eighty percent of people over age 60. But not all are due to age. Babies can be born with cataracts, and some develop from injuries, drugs, or other causes.

The brightest news in the picture, however, lies in the modern-day treatment. In the past, cataract surgery meant hospitalization and lengthy recuperation. Today, the vast majority of cases are handled as outpatients. In most instances, an artificial "intraocular" lens is implanted after the natural lens of the eye is surgically removed. Actual surgery time is from 20 to 45 minutes, and the individual returns to normal activities very quickly.

So at six o'clock in the morning on a recent day, I found myself, accompanied by Momma, reporting to the hospital.

First, a brief session in the admissions office, then on to a room where I'd be prepared for surgery. Everything moved calmly, smoothly.

And just before a bandage was placed over my eye, I took a last look through my natural lens in my left eye. I looked down at my slippered feet. There they were, fuzzy and blurred. And I knew I wasn't making a mistake.

Today, cataract surgeries are normally done with local anesthetics. But patients can ask for more. And I had. I would receive an added little "bump" of a sedative intravenously.

And finally the moment of truth as I was wheeled under a sign marked "Surgery." A pause, a final word, a squeeze of the hand by Momma, and I was on my way.

The surgery was a piece of cake. Conscious through it all, relaxed, I listened to the voices of my doctor and the other attendants, to soft piano music piped from above. A short hour later, I was back in my room, resting, preparing to return to the motel with Momma.

And the anxious moment the next day, my first post-operative check, when the bandage came off and I tested my "new eye" for the first time. A quick glance at the wall chart gave me assurance. Where I hadn't been able to read even the largest letter at the top, now I could read the second line from the bottom, letters maybe a half-inch high.

Truly a miracle! And a wave of relief and gratitude swept through me.

Things are going just fine, thank you!

March, 1993

# Charlie Cool Grants An Interview

The guy doesn't give out many interviews, that's for sure. Not that he's temperamental, like some ego-struck movie star. It's just that he's busy. He's got things on his mind, things to do.

But he gave me some time the other evening. Not a whole lot, just enough to ask a few questions. And while he was obviously bored by my nosiness, he was polite, courteous, with his answers.

I'm talking about Charlie Cool, one of my grandson buddies. Now, folks that have read these words of mine over the years know that his real name is Kyle. But from almost birth on, I've tagged him else-wise. Because of his independent personality.

Well, Charlie's seven now, about to start the second grade. And he and his younger brother, Jesse (Mighty Cool), just accompanied their mother out east on a two-week trip to visit relatives, to places like New York and Maine; a journey that covered almost 4,000 miles, if you count all the side trips to ice cream shops and water slides.

And the other night, on their return, Grandma and I drove over to welcome them home. Charlie was glad to see us, hiding behind a door as we entered, to leap out and wrap us both in his best hugs.

His mom proceeded to tell us that Charlie'd learned to

read road signs. And how excited he'd gotten on the way home, as they'd passed the welcome sign at the Wisconsin-Michigan border.

Her words led me to think that Charlie would be brim-full of news. Not quite. Brim-full of pent-up energy, yes! News, no! And off he went with Mighty to ride their bikes on the driveway.

Well, being the persistent digger of information that I am, I followed. Pulling up a lawn chair, I began my questions, hoping Charlie'd take time to answer.

"Tell me about your trip," I said, opening our interview. "What happened?"

"Well, I learned to swim," he answered. "In a lake! Actually it was the ocean." (True, his mom verified later.)

"Tell me about Niagara Falls," I asked. "I know you spent a day there."

"Oh," he said, matter-of-factly, "it was beautiful. We went on a boat ride and we got wet (from the mist). And we went to some haunted houses (a wax museum). My brother was scared."

At that point, Mom appeared with the souvenirs they'd chosen. A backscratcher for Mighty and a fur coonskin cap for Charlie. "It was ninety degrees, but he wore it all the time we were there," she laughed.

"How about New York City? Tell me about the Empire State Building," I continued, addressing Charlie.

"It was high... VERY high," he answered. "We took an elevator to the top. It was kinda scary. There's ten or eleven stories, I guess." (Actually 102 Mom told.)

"And you could see the Statue of Liberty from up there. What did that look like?" I pursued.

"Well, it's kinda like a statue of a king with his hand up in the air," Charlie explained. "And he's holding a stick with some fire on it." Not a bad description, I thought, even though the king happens to be a queen.

"And the Bronx Zoo, what did you see there?"

A resigned sigh and a deep breath. I could see I was getting too pushy.

"Just plain old animals and stuff," he replied, calling on all his patience. "I saw a live gorilla, and a lazy old lion, and a big old elephant." Nothing particularly impressive to Charlie apparently.

And with that, he retreated to ride his green three-wheeler tractor down the blacktop. No more questions. The interview was over.

But a final Charlie Coolism from Mom.

Seems Charlie got his first taste of lobster at a restaurant along the coast of Maine and liked it, polishing off a big two-pounder. On doing so he proudly announced, "I could've eaten two of those!"

That's my Charlie buddy!

August, 1993

# Cool As Cucumbers

"Whoo! It's sure going to be a cooker today!" one of my uncles would say as our farm work day would begin. High above, a blazing sun would glow from a cloudless, blue sky.

Heat waves! Hot spells! Cookers! Call them what you will. The one we experienced recently in mid-July was a dandy. Temperatures in the high nineties, even over one hundred! Heat that broke records throughout the Midwest.

But around our place it'll be the last of those ordeals! Never again will Momma and I argue about whether the windows of our house should be open or shut when it's hot outside! For even as I write, the finishing touches are being put on a central air conditioning system.

It's a luxury that I never dreamed I'd enjoy. And as Momma and I sat talking the other day about how wonderful it's going to be, both of us got to reminiscing... about how things were when we were kids and it got hot, about how folks coped back then.

"Remember the ice man?" I said to her. And together we exchanged memories about the little square cardboard sign our mothers would place in a front window facing the street. Around its edge would be numbers, like 25 and 50. The card would be positioned so that the figure at the top represented the poundage of ice you wished to order.

Sometime during the day, a truck would stop in the street. Out would step its husky driver. And with a set of tongs, from the back of the truck he'd grasp a huge chunk of ice, flip it onto his pad-covered shoulder, walk through the back door, and deposit the chunk with a thud into the top of the ice box in mother's kitchen.

If we were lucky, a sliver would break off, a cold treat for one of us kids to savor.

Those old ice boxes served to keep food cool before refrigerators came along. Today they're antiques. And rightly so, because some of them were beautifully crafted of polished oak and steel.

"Remember the Sammy men?" Momma chuckled. "I suppose parents hated them!" Sammy men sold ice cream bars. A nickel, the bars cost. Not much today, but in the 1930's, folks watched their nickels.

Sammy men rode three-wheeled white bicycles with insulated boxes mounted at the rear. On the handlebars was a little bell that could be rung with his thumb.

Sammy men were smart. They knew where all the kids in the neighborhood lived. And as one slowly pedalled his way, he knew exactly when to pause to ring his bell. A couple of well-spaced "chings" and kids would come running like flushed-out rabbits, clutching their nickels. While their poor mothers agonized between love for their kids and balancing the family budget!

"Remember the swimsuits hanging on the clothesline after we'd run through the sprinkler in the back yard?" Momma continued. "And neighbors sitting outside in the evenings, visiting together, trying to cool off. You don't see much of that any more!"

And memories of my own, like summers spent on my grandfather's farm in the late 30's, times of extreme heat and drought. So severe that I vividly recall our church filled with sun-browned farm folks on Sunday mornings, bowing their heads in unison to openly pray for rain, moisture needed to save their crops.

Too, I remember long days in my Grandpa's cornfields, bare-footed, with only a straw hat between my head and the burning sun, hoeing thistles. Grandpa hated thistles, and I was dispatched to rid his farm of the dastardly weeds whenever he found a patch.

There I'd work, the sun beating down from above, its heat radiating off the black earth around me, chopping thistles. I've always said that I burned out my body's thermostat in my grand-father's cornfields. Never since have I been able to tolerate heat very well!

And the nights! Let darkness fall, and what little breeze there might be would die. The upstairs bedrooms of the farm house would be stifling. Many was the time I joined my uncles and aunts as they carried blankets and pillows down the hall, and out-side, to sleep on the grass of the lawn. Anything to beat the heat.

But those are all just old memories now. Momma and I are entering a new era, a time of modern-day luxury.

Some time ago I wrote in this column about some of the real-ly great inventions that have come along in my lifetime, things like ball-point pens, automatic chokes on cars, and unbreakable thermos bottles.

I now add to that list air conditioning. Let that next heat wave come, I say! Momma's going to set the thermostat, or whatever they call the gadget that controls the temperature... and we're both going to sit back cool as cucumbers.

I can hear myself now.

"Aaah! Pass me some more of that good lemonade, please!" I'll be a-sayin'!

August, 1995

# A Passion For Tractors

Down memory lane, Gene Wisner was taking me. That's how I felt as he showed me around his collection of memorabilia from times long ago.

Past an old Maytag washing machine with a gasoline-powered motor, a machine exactly like the one my mother once used. Past an early-day gas engine with two huge flywheels, just like the one that once powered my grandfather's little sawmill. And old bottles, hub caps, wrenches and more.

But best of all, the old tractors. Wisner, you see, collects and restores old tractors... John Deere tractors, to be exact. He's got seventeen in the big storage shed behind his Spooner home.

And therein lies a story of a man and his love for machines.

Wisner's 67 now, and he's been retired since 1986, put to pasture from a long career with the Beloit Corporation where he helped make and install paper-making machinery. Along the way, he'd also worked as a mechanic. And those jobs honed his knowledge of now mechanical things work and should be repaired.

His passion for tractors was born long before those working days, however.

"It started in the late 30's when I and Jim Donatell would

work after school for his father, Frank. Frank had a John Deere dealership in Spooner, and he'd give us a few quarters to clean up old machinery."

"There weren't many tractors around these parts then. Farmers used horses. Frank would go out and talk to farmers about tractors. Most said they didn't think tractors were here to stay. But they soon learned how much work could be saved."

After that first spark as a youngster, Wisner's interest in tractors laid dormant until 1982. "Then one day while living in Beloit, I happened to go to a Thrasheree at Edgerton where they had old tractors, steam engines and old-time farm machinery. That's when the bug hit me. I had to have a tractor," Gene said.

"I heard about one for sale at Spooner, and I bought it. I hauled it all the way back to Beloit," he added. "And in 1986 when I retired and moved back to Spooner, I had to bring that old tractor back too. It's a 1930 John Deere Model GP, which stands for 'general purpose'. It was the first model built that could plow and cultivate, and had a power take-off and belt pulley on it."

And with that his tractor collecting became more intense.

"Eva, my wife, and I spend our winters in Arizona," Gene continued. "There I ran across a Model B in mint condition except for its paint. Well, I had to buy it, and I also had to buy a pickup to bring it home!"

"The next one came from Louisiana, another Model B," he said. "It had skeleton wheels for working in the rice fields. And I had to buy a trailer to bring IT home!"

Today, in Wisner's shed, his tractors rest in various stages of restoration. He works on two or three at a time. Most have something wrong with them when he acquires them. The

*Gene Wisner restores antique tractors.*

most common fault is piston and cylinder damage from poor maintenance.

"You have to be careful," Wisner said. "I fill the head with penetrating oil, then use a sledge hammer or a hydraulic press to free the pistons. I seldom break one. Those old tractors had heavy cast-iron pistons."

Exteriors of all parts are sand-blasted and painted with John Deere green and yellow before re-assembly.

Parts are still obtainable for more recent models, like his 1949 and 1951 machines. Others he gets from antique tractor salvage yards. He spends about 200 hours on each tractor.

And why does he do it?

"It's a hobby," Wisner says. "I've never sold a tractor. My goal is to bring them back to life, so they look like they did when they were new."

"One of the things I like is the history," he went on. "Tractors accelerated the agricultural and industrial revolution. People don't realize how many hours of labor went into making a tractor, all the way from the mining of the iron ore to the manufacture in a factory."

"It's really gratifying for me to take something that's all rusty and been sitting out in the weeds in a field for thirty years and bring it back to life. People come by to look at them and talk. Just the other day some folks from Virginia stopped. Their son, they said, is a John Deere collector too."

And with that he proceeded to start his old 1935 Model B, turning on the gas, setting the choke, and spinning the fly wheel. The engine coughed once, then sputtered to life with a lyrical "putt-putt-putt", and settled into the smooth rhythmic sound that only an old John Deere can make.

...music to the ears of both of us.

June, 1994

# Valentines

Valentine's Day comes at the right time of the year, I say. What with our cold northern winters, we can sure use a warm hug or two by the time that sweet-talk holiday rolls around.

Valentines came up for some heavy discussion around our house recently. Momma had been down in the basement tackling a winter project. There she was rummaging around in what I call our "junk" room.

And down from a shelf came two old cardboard boxes, their sides darkened by time. Boxes that had been passed on to us many years ago. Boxes that we've faithfully shuffled from house to house and town to town as we've travelled the roads of life.

"Can you believe these?" she announced, coming up the basement stairs, her hands laden with packets of papers. And she proceeded to lay in front of me schoolwork from her childhood. Old report cards, sheets of arithmetic, and simple stories she'd written in grade school.

And immediately, the nostalgia of those 1930-times swept over both of us.

"Look at this!" she said. And she held aloft one of those old-fashioned cardboard fans that folks used many years ago to cool their brows, before electric fans and air conditioning came along. But a special old fan, one with a picture of the

Dionne Quintuplets on it... five little girls resting in their baby chairs playing with their dollies.

"And this!" Momma went on, holding up an aged kid's coloring book. "I must have been about four!" A special book with Shirley Temple's face as a child on its cover! Glancing through it, I chided her for not staying inside the lines sometimes... as I've done with our own kids and grandkids.

"But these are really something!" she exclaimed, opening a small cardboard box. Inside were a couple dozen old valentines. And one by one she examined each, savoring the messages and feelings that each carried.

Many were hand-made, some when she was very young obviously, evident by their crudeness. Then others more elaborate with big red hearts cut from construction paper and glued to lace-like paper doilies to add beauty and finesse. "To Daddy" and "To Mother" the more fancy read. Some made from wallpaper samples cut and pasted by child fingers into simple designs. And a mix of the penny-a-piece variety that came from dime stores, valentines from friends; Raymond, Richard, and Earl. And Jean and Jane and Grandma.

"What was Valentine's Day like at your school?" I asked. Quickly that led into a trip down memory lane.

"I always got to make the box that we put our valentines in," she said. "Because I always volunteered first! My mother often said I was born with my right hand in the air!"

She made the box at home, she said. "I made glue out of flour and water and pasted red hearts and paper doilies on it. And I made ruffles from crepe paper. Off to school I'd go, proudly carrying it!"

The afternoon of Valentine's Day, the box would be

opened. "There was always a lot of anticipation over who you were giving valentines to, and who you'd get them from," Momma told. "Your greatest fear was not getting any. It was always a great relief when you got some."

The boys, it seemed, often sent each other valentines that had 'nasty' sayings on them. "You were always happy when you didn't get one of those," Momma said. "But the boys were glad when they did!"

Then, there was always a special hand-made one for her teacher, she added.

There'd be some candy, red spicy hearts, a treat from the teacher. "It was a big deal to get a couple pieces," she said. "Of course, you always got a piece in the valentine from your special friend. And you always put one in hers."

Too, those boxes on the basement shelf contained some other treasures, old books. And later, after our valentine talk, I looked them over. Titles like "Heidi", "The Campfire Girls", and "Five Little Peppers and How They Grew." Books that were classics for girls in the 1930's. Books that were presents for birthdays, Christmases and graduations. Books that carry a lot of emotion to this day for Momma.

But none quite reach the level of meaning that her old valentines do.

...That's why they were saved so many years ago, I'm sure.

February, 1996

# Λ Class "Λ" Winter

Hey! I just might make it! I just might get through the winter without having to shovel the snow from our roof.

As of this writing, sure there's still a half a foot of the white stuff up there. But it's going fast. And with spring only a few days away, at least on the calendar, I'm cautiously optimistic. I say cautiously, because we all know how fickle March can be.

Anyway, for the last six weeks or so, I've been eyeing both my roof and the weather forecasts; calculating my chances of not having to climb up there, to engage in the thrilling ritual of pushing the snow over the edge, to listen to the rotten stuff cascade with a thud to the ground below.

Well, it looks like I'm going to luck out.

Which means that we've had a Class A winter!

I have this rating system for winters, you see. Three classes: A, B and C. A Class A winter is one that requires no roof shovelling. A Class B rating means one such clearing. And Class C applies to winters when two clearings are necessary, winters that are the pits.

Last year, 1991, for example, was a Class C winter. In fact, I came close to adding a new category, Class D! (Da worst!)

Now I know that a lot of people don't believe in clearing snow from their roofs. An acquaintance and I were once discussing that question, and he offered an interesting opinion on the subject. "The Good Lord put that snow up there," my friend said, "and He can take it down."

But I'm not so sure about divine intervention when I look up and see two feet of the stuff bearing down on my bedroom. And it's then that I slip into some longjohns and my ice fishing clothes, place a ladder against the eaves, and gingerly step onto the slippery shingles. Getting up on the roof safely is half the battle. The other half is getting down. And I don't mean unintentionally, like over the side with a scoop of snow.

Over the years, I've experimented with several snow-clearing tools. Like the old-fashioned snow shovel for instance. A lot of people use those. But they're a lot of bending, and they move only a little snow with each bite. Besides, one has to work awfully close to the roof's edge, something that I don't like, being that I have a high center of gravity and tend to be on the ungraceful side.

So I made what I call a snow "pusher." Momma had bought some carpeting, and in it was a hefty, twelve-foot length of bamboo, a perfect handle. To which I firmly attached a piece of lumber. The gadget worked very well. Still, it was heavy and cumbersome.

And I moved on to one of those sheet metal snow scoops that you push. Well, the thing worked OK. It could move a lot of snow with each push. But at the end of each, at the roof's edge, I'd have to give the scoop a little snap to send the snow flying over the side. A couple times the scoop slipped out of my wet gloves, sailing off into space too, with the snow.

So back to the drawing board! I'm proud to say that I believe I have finally invented the ultimate in roof snow-clearing tools. Down to the hardware store I went, purchasing one of those curved lightweight aluminum snow scrapers. Then to the lumber yard for a ten-foot chunk of some of that round stair railing.

Back home, I removed the handle that came with the scraper and replaced it with the piece of stair railing. Well, my ingenious invention has proven to be a great success! I can stand up there on the roof and push snow with the greatest of ease. And safely back from the roof's edge.

But not this year. We've had a Class A winter!

And I have to confess that I feel a twinge of regret inside. I can't say that I ever actually enjoyed clearing my roof. Still, there's a certain satisfaction in this north country that comes from meeting winter on its own terms, and facing it down.

But I can live with that melancholy, especially now that my old sweetheart, Miz Spring, is courting me once more; flirting and fluttering her eyelashes seductively across the countryside.

Oh, I know she's around. She waltzed through the backyard the other day, causing Butch, my dog, to emerge from his house to squat contentedly on his little porch, to soak up her warm sunshine. And I've seen her several times out on the lakes where the bluegill fishermen sit on their pails with their jackets open and mittens off.

And that sweet little thing is blowing her soft breezes over my roof, melting the blanket of white that's been there since November, bringing it slowly earthward in tiny rivlets that trickle from the downspouts.

She's doing a good job, one that I didn't need to do.

Give me a good old Class A winter any time!

March, 1993

# The Spirit Of Christmas

Christmas is still a few days in the offing as I write. Around me, and elsewhere, the Christmas spirit burns warmly. Though Christmas will be past by the time these words appear, its spirit, I expect, will still be burning brightly.

I've been on a search these recent days, a quest of sorts, to find the spirit of Christmas. Christmas, after all, is more than a holiday on the calendar. Christmas has meaning and purpose, substance that adds value to our lives.

So I've been searching for the spirit of Christmas; quietly, casually, subtly, in my daily activities. I've looked and I've listened, hoping to savor such spirit wherever I could find it.

And indeed, find it I did.

There it was in a country church, for instance. It's a church I pass a hundred times a year. Lately, however, for some reason, it's taken on a different aura.

There it stands, stately, dignified, on a snow-decked hilltop, serene; the early morning sunlight reflecting from its stained-glass windows. Reaching for the heavens is a tall white steeple. And in that tower hangs an old bell, poised to peal its message across the countryside on Christmas day that the birthday of Christ is about to be celebrated.

There's perpetuity in that old church, I decide. Strength that seems to say that good will in mankind will prevail, even in our darkest hours.

Down the road a ways, a trout stream flows, its waters eddying black against the snow-covered marsh through which it passes. The scene is peaceful and tranquil. And in that peace and tranquility, I find too the spirit of Christmas. Peace on earth, after all, is a strong message of Christmas.

And then, one morning, while Harold Henriksen and I were moving out some Christmas trees out at the tree farm, there on an old stone fence, three ruffed grouse sat perched, eyeing us as we went about our work. There they were, resplendent in their mottled gray-brown plumage, the morning sun shining on their speckled breasts.

There too, in those birds, I found a bit of the spirit of Christmas. For in them, and my pine trees into which they eventually flew, trees that I planted, I find love. Love for the land and the wondrous things it nourishes if given a chance. Love for the life it supports. Life upon which we mortals depend for our very sustenance.

I found the spirit of Christmas in people.

I found it in the excitement of our North Carolina gang as they announced over the phone that they'd be coming home for Christmas. And I found it in the voices of our Hayward gang as they described how they'd cut the family tree, then toasted hot dogs over a fire they built.

For in those things are joy, one of the prime ingredients of Christmas.

And I found it, in the warm gloves I received from the parents of a little girl, a youngster that I wanted to give a Christmas tree to, and did. It's in the exchange of gifts such as that, where the giving replenishes the giver, that the heart of Christmas lies.

Then, I found Christmas spirit in the dozens of small

towns and villages, some barely cross-road hamlets, through which I passed. Where the symbols of Christmas hung from roadside poles and street lights. Long ropes of evergreen boughs, tinsel candy canes, red bells and silver stars, all intended to brighten the hearts of passer-bys.

Yes, I found the spirit of Christmas in many places. Some here, a little there. But nowhere in the totality like I did a recent day.

...There she was, dressed in a blue snowsuit, about eight years old I'd say. I saw her for some distance as I approached, about to pass by her country home with my load of Christmas trees. There she was, preparing to slide down a snowbank on her plastic toboggan sled.

And as I passed, she began to wave. Not just a weak little wave, but big happy waves with both hands, back and forth high above her head. Across her face spread a big happy smile.

There, I said to myself, is the spirit of Christmas that I've been looking for. There in that joyful, innocent, vibrant, sharing child was the true meaning of Christmas.

...After all, that's how it all had begun, I thought... with a child.

December, 1994

# Carving Totem Poles

Back in 1992, when I learned that Leo Root was retiring, I stopped at the store he'd managed in Spooner for many years. I wanted to wish him well, and over a cup of coffee, I did.

The other day, I found myself again sipping coffee with Leo, this time in the comfortable secluded home that he and his wife, Corrine, share on Ellsworth Lake. There I listened as he told me about a new chapter in his life... an unusual retirement hobby, that of carving totem poles.

He's made three. And one, a handsome ten-footer, stands on his lawn to overlook the lake.

Root's interest in totem poles stems from time that he and Corrine spent in Alaska. "We went up there in 1954," he said. "I'd just got out of the Army, and a friend invited us to come up. I had an old Dodge truck, and we took off. It was a rough trip, 3400 miles. I used 15 quarts of oil and 15 tires!"

In Anchorage, Root looked for work and landed a job with an oil company refueling airplanes. "I worked for them for eight years," he said.

And during that time, he learned about the totem poles that Alaska's Native American people had carved for centuries.

"The poles tell a story," Leo said. "They tell a family's history and they provide identification for the family. For

Leo Root carves totem poles as a hobby.

example, if the family were fishermen, the pole might show a bear holding a salmon. According to tradition the poles aren't supposed to be maintained.

"I've always had a fascination with Indian culture," he added. "It's really fascinating to me to see what they could do with what they had to work with!

"I got interested in making totem poles when I retired. I'd always wanted one, but I didn't have time to make it. I had an old telephone pole, so I said what the heck, and I took it into the basement and got started."

He also bought a book called "How to Carve and Paint Totem Poles." Authored by Paul N. Luvera of Washington state, the book's data and instructions have been helpful.

The carving is done in the basement of his home. "If I'd known I was going to get into this, I'd have designed my basement differently when I built our house," he said.

He works on the poles only in the winter, from November to March. He'll make one per winter, he says. A finished totem requires about 200 hours of his time.

Old cedar telephone poles that he secures locally are his raw material. "It's hard to get a good one because of the knots and tar," he noted.

Once the log is in place on sawhorses, the carving begins. "I use hand tools like chisels and rasps," he said, "though I do have an electric chain saw and a little Dremel power tool. You've got to have a hammer. I finally bought myself a carver's mallet with a rubber head. The work takes a lot of muscle!

"Dust is a problem. All my tools have dust catchers, and I wear a mask. But they do get uncomfortable."

Root carefully scales out the images that he wants on the pole, faces of animals and birds, eagles, bears, fish and beaver. "Patience is something you really have to have," he noted. "I'm getting quite a bit better. I've laid awake at night trying to figure out how to solve a problem. You just don't know until you start hacking away! You can't go at it too fast."

An image is not intended to look exactly like an animal. Instead it depicts a more mystical appearance.

As with most creative work, Root works best when the mood strikes him, sometimes working right through his lunch time. "You can't just go down there for 15 minutes," he said. "You have to stick with it."

When the carving is finished, the pole is treated with two

coats of water-repellent preservative. And finally painted with bright exterior latex paint or stain, all brushed on by hand.

The second and third poles that Root made were quickly bought by people eager to own a totem. So has the pole that's currently under construction. "I do it primarily for the fun," he says. "You can only have so many totem poles in your yard!"

Little did I know four years ago that a cup of coffee with Leo Root would lead to another... and an interesting retirement pastime.

Like making totem poles.

November, 1996

# Knee-Moania

Ouch! Oooo...! Ow!

Folks, that's the kind of life I've been leading lately. For the past two months, I've been living a lie, telling the world how much fun I've been having traipsing around the lakes ice-fishing, enjoying leisurely walks in the woods, and other good stuff.

Ouch! Whew! (I was hurting.)

All that time I was faking it, pulling your leg, so to speak. And now it's time to 'fess up. That cheery, brave front was all just an act.

Ouch! Bleep! Bleep! (That's how I really felt.)

The past few weeks haven't been the best of times, that's for sure. Now it's time to set the record straight with you fine folks. And as for my subterfuge, I haven't got a leg to stand on!

I've had a bum knee, you see. People close to me... Momma, the family, friends, they've known about it. But not the rest of the world.

I call it a case of "knee-moania." Why? Well, first because it's a knee, my left, that's been hurting. And second, because the pain has caused me to do a lot of moaning. In private, that is.

So what's the big deal about a boogered knee, you ask. Let me explain. I'm known for my philosophy on dealing with ailments. I rely heavily on a "do-it-myself, let-Mother-Nature-take-its-course" approach.

Well, I tried that. Which didn't work. Which sent me to the doctor's office. Which is what I should have done in the first place.

There, to make a long story short, the x-rays and the MRI (magnetic resonance imagery) exam pinpointed the cause of my aches, a torn cartilage. Which is a fairly common sort of a knee injury these days, especially if you're a professional football player, or perhaps a senior citizen line dancer.

Which brought me to the wonderful world of modern-day arthroscopic surgery, a good news scenario if I've ever heard one.

But through those two months that it took me to reach that point, came considerable soul-searching. Why had I boogered my knee? And where and when?

I'm the kind of a guy who values his legs. I've relied on them for a lifetime in the outdoors. My legs are responsible for my lifestyle. And without them, I wasn't sure that there could be another lifestyle.

All my life, I've been a walker, I came to conclude. From early age on, when I first explored the far corners of my grandfathers' farms, deciphering the secrets of the birds and animals that lived there. To a lifetime in the forestry and conservation business, work that allowed me to peek into a good bit of northern Wisconsin's remote back country.

And to today's retirement years and their casual satisfactions... wading lonely trout streams, sneaking brushy grouse trails, and culturing crops of trees.

How had I done myself in, I asked. Perhaps a hundred ways, places and times, I decided. A trip on the snowshoes, a slip out at the tree farm, a twist in a trout stream.

Overexertion on a dance floor? Not likely!!

And so, a few days ago, the surgery was performed. Not many years ago, the procedure would have involved a substantial incision and a lengthy recuperation period.

Not today. At least not for me. Three little incisions, so small they can be covered with Band-Aids. Then, using a remarkable instrument called an arthroscope, my good doctor surgeon located and repaired the two cartilage tears that were the source of the problem.

All done with out-patient surgery, which meant that I could enter the hospital in late morning and be home for supper that night.

Discomfort? None, really, at least for me. Unless you count a couple of days of crutch use or the thrill of an ice pack against your bare skin.

Restrictions? "Just don't get too frisky right away," my doctor said.

By the time these words reach print, I expect to be back to full speed once more. And it's going to feel great!

The moan will be gone from my "knee-monia"!

February, 1995

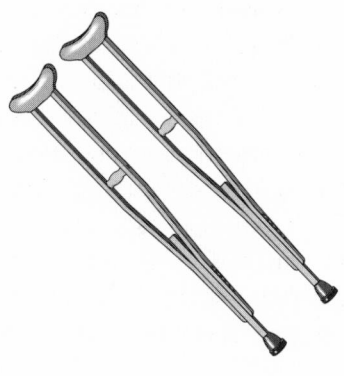

# History At Their Doorstep

A lot of Wisconsin history lies at the doorstep of the home of Glen and Lorraine Crosby... literally.

There, in the valley of the Clam River west of Shell Lake, Chippewa Indian people passed long ago in their birchbark canoes. Early trappers roamed, seeking the furs of beaver, mink, and muskrat. And rugged lumberjacks rode big pine logs as they drove their winter's cut downstream to Minnesota sawmills.

The valley was taking on a touch of springtime, as I visited with Glen and Lorraine. The wooded hills were finally free of snow; and pastures, where cattle rested, were showing their first blush of green. A pair of cardinals, spectacular in their brilliant red coats, flitted in the Crosby yard.

Built on a high knoll overlooking a sharp bend of the river, the home, now remodeled, has a long and colorful history.

"The house was built in 1875 as a stopping place for loggers," Glen told. "It was built by Jack Arbuckle as a rooming house.

"This is what the place used to look like," he continued, handing me an old photograph showing himself as a three-year-old in 1928 standing in front of the three-storied, gabled, white-frame structure.

"It had a saloon right here," he said, pointing. "I tore that off myself. The third story was a dance hall. People walked all the way from Clam Falls to come to the dances. The floors were worn down from the hobnail boots the loggers wore."

"There were 23 rooms in the house," Lorraine added. "And three chimneys, two starting on the third floor. Stove pipes ran through the walls. It was surprising that it didn't burn down."

"The old barn was probably built before the house," Glen said. "It's got big hand-hewn timbers. The wood shingles were about 100 years old. When we got here, there was a blacksmith shop where they shod horses and did repair work. And there used to be a hitching post down by the chicken house."

The Crosbys remember the old tote roads that wound through the valley to the logging camps. Today they're hard to find.

"I remember my dad having a hired man who was an old-timer," Glen said. "He told how he used to put hay on the frozen ice roads to slow down the sleigh loads of logs."

The Crosbys recently celebrated their 50th wedding anniversary. "All in this house," Glen said. "We raised six kids here, all good citizens." One son now operates a nearby dairy farm with Glen helping, though two surgeries, a hip replacement and a shoulder replacement, limit his activities somewhat.

"We've seen some hard times," Glen said. "And with the farm prices now, we're seeing them again."

And some memories of what the valley was like in years past.

"After the pine was cut, the woods burned. My dad said you could drive anywhere with a team of horses," Glen noted. "When I was a kid this country had lots of pheasants and sharptail grouse."

And recollections of how the foxes and coyotes multiplied to prey on their chickens and sheep.

I asked about trout fishing on the Clam, a well-known stream.

"The river's in bad shape now because of the beavers," Glen replied. "I used to like to see the trout fishermen come. I got to know a lot of them as I pulled them out when they'd get stuck in the frost boils. Now there's only a few, and they're gone in a little while. I hope the high water takes out the beaver dams."

And some reminiscing about the tough times of the Depression years.

"My folks would drive to Shell Lake. They always had to fix flat tires on the way," Glen said. "My mother decided they'd buy new tires for the car... one a year at $3 apiece!"

"Our mail carrier was Art Rounce," he went on. "In winter he had a Model T with tracks over the wheels, like a snowmobile. He was also one of the best fiddle players that ever lived. He'd drop off the mail and play a couple tunes. Then he'd be on his way."

"I had a pony that just loved tobacco," Glen said. "He'd nip at a fisherman's pocket if there was a box of snuff in it. One night a fisherman had a cigar in his mouth. All at once something snapped it right out of his mouth, scaring him half to death. There was my pony!"

A lot of water has gone down the Clam in the years that the Crosbys have lived on its banks. Soon the yellow marsh marigolds and the blue violets will bloom along its way, as they have for centuries.

I stood at the river's edge with Glen and Lorraine the

other day, and I half-expected to hear the echo of a whoop from an old-time lumberjack riding a big pine log down the river.

Instead we listened to the laughter of a rapids as it swirled before us.

"I've always liked that sound," I heard Glen say.

A sound that's always been special to me too.

May, 1996

*Glen and Lorraine Crosby live on the Historic Clam River.*

# A River For Boys

April's a bitter-sweet month, we all know... a mixed-up mess of warm sunshine and wild snowstorms. Calendar-wise, it's a time of adolescence. April can't quite seem to make up its mind as to what it wants to do, or what it wants to be. It's a time when we live on the ragged edge of winter and the rugged edge of spring.

But, most of all, April's a time of birth and awakening, of new life around us and revived spirit within us.

Never were those feelings stronger than in my boyhood!

Let the melting snowbanks send their rivlets of water down the ditches of my country road, let me shed my heavy winter mackinaw, let my feet touch soft bare earth once again, and my heart would lead me to pasture creeks and backwoods ponds, to explore and ponder the secrets of nature.

There I'd lie on my belly and watch crayfish scurry in the rocks of a stream bottom. There, I'd slip off my heavy work shoes and wade barefooted into mucky waters to dip beady strings of frogs' eggs into mason jars borrowed from my mother's basement canning supplies.

As the warmer days of May neared, however, my thoughts would once more stir. With my curiosity staved for the new life bursting around me, satisfied by newly-built nests and freshly-dug burrows, a new appetite would begin to burn within me. And my mind would drift to fishing, of rippling water and bullheads and sunfish.

The hunger would grow; and when it no longer could be denied, I'd begin the sharing of my dream with my younger brother, Bill, and my neighborhood buddies. To no surprise, boys being boys, I found that they too felt my yearning. And with heads huddled on back porch steps, we'd plan our first fishing trip of the year.

...to the Pike River.

As rivers go, the Pike wasn't all that much. Maybe thirty feet across at its widest, at no place too deep for us to wade; in the world of rivers, it was at best a lightweight. But to country kids used to jumping puny 'cricks' in cow pastures, it was the mother of all waters. And we revered it, at least for a few of our growing-up years.

And so, an expedition would be organized. Bamboo and willow fish poles were checked. Perhaps a missing fish hook replaced. Maybe a new stringer manufactured from a strong piece of line and a ten-penny nail from the tool shed. And an assumed "blessing" cleared with our folks to be gone for a day from our farm chores.

The trip, you see, would take a full day, the river being some four miles distant. Today, I shake my head in disbelief that our parents would let us kids, youngsters barely eight and ten years old, go off alone on such an adventure. But go we did, and never once did we get into trouble.

Early morning would find the half-dozen of us hiking along the gravel roads north toward the Pike. Over our shoulders, under our arms, and in our pockets were the fish poles, the worm-filled bait cans, and the lunches, usually homemade bread sandwiches, that we'd need for the day.

The long walk seemed to take forever. But hastened by

strong, farm-toughened legs and visions of pools where hungry fish awaited, the miles eventually passed. And finally, that glorious moment when we could plunge down a bank to our favorite rock, unwind our lines, thread on a full-bodied earthworm, and cast out our baited hooks.

There we'd spend the day, watching for a bullhead or a sunfish to jiggle our corks, stolen from old vinegar jugs that grandpa would use for drinking water come haying time.

Ah, but that was living! We never caught many fish. A bullhead or two and a sunfish on a stringer was a good catch. And never big. A six-incher was worth bragging about. Unless, of course, you were lucky enough to tie into a foot-long sucker.

Get your line snagged on a rock or root, and wade out to free the precious hook. No water was too cold to risk losing a hook. And never did scrambled egg sandwiches taste better than eaten on a rock next to moving water, with good-natured boy chatter ringing through the trees.

Nightfall would find us straggling home... wet, sunburned, shoes muddy, overalls torn, hungry, exhuasted, but basking in the glow of a great fishing trip.

Our parents seemed to understand, as I recall.

After all, boys will be boys.

April, 1995

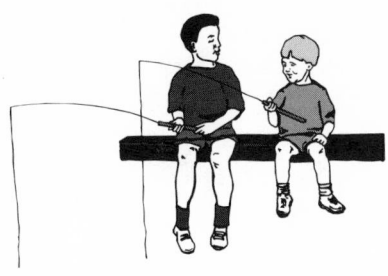

# Matthew, My Mean Machine

"Looks like it's a day for Matthew!" I say to Momma these mornings, as I look out the window at a blanket of new snow that carpets the driveway.

Matthew is my new snowblower, the red-and-black mean machine that I bought last fall after selling my old one at Momma's rummage sale.

Matthew? Name a snowblower Matthew? This guy Becker has finally lost it! I know what you're thinking, loyal readers!

Well see, it's this way. I've had this habit all my life, that of giving names to machines of mine... everything from tractors to deer rifles! But only after the machine displays a certain personality... and we get on a first-name basis based on that personality.

That's how my new snowblower got its name. I came up with "Matthew" after we'd had a chance to get to know each other, after working side by side a couple times, to blast our common enemy, snow, to bits.

That's when good ol' Matt displayed the sturdy stuff that he's made of. Wheel the guy out of the garage, fill his gas tank, open the gas line, set the choke, advance the throttle, push the primer button a couple times, and give the starter rope a hefty pull!

Bingo! With a mighty roar, Matthew coughs to life,

announcing to Enemy Snow that it had better be ready for battle!

Crank the chute to the side so that the white stuff lands on the lawn, not the front porch! Slip the gear shift lever into place, turn on the auger, give Matthew his head, and down the driveway we go; fearlessly, relentlessly tearing Enemy Snow to shreds, chomping and chewing and spitting his remains off into space!

Ah, yes! It became obvious after an experience or two like that that my snowblower needed a name that smacked of masculinity, one that conveyed an image of strength and toughness. That's why I came up with Matthew! Matthew's a strong and tough name in my book.

Down the driveway, the two of us march! In my mind, I feel like one of General George Patton's tank drivers back in World War II, busting through a German panzer unit in the Battle of the Bulge!

Hit 'em in the gut, I tell good ol' Matt. And down through the belly of Enemy Snow, we slice a wide swath, inflicting a mortal wound, sending Enemy back on his heels, reeling in pain.

Then a brilliant maneuver as we emerge from the driveway onto the street. With a flourish of Matthew's transmission, his knobby tires spin as we reverse direction with a deft pirouette, sending us up Enemy Snow's flank... catching the dastardly fiend completely off guard, cutting off his supply line of drifting stuff being carried in on the north wind.

Ah, I'm telling you, it's beautiful to watch Matthew in action. Up and down the driveway we churn, Matt totally disemboweling Enemy.

And only in third gear!

That's something else about Matthew. He's got power to

spare! Six speeds forward, for example! So far I've only had nerve enough to run him in third gear! Like the old cars I had back in my youth, I'm afraid to run him "wide open"!

Heck, I can barely keep up with him in third. What if I turned him up to number six? Not knowing his strength, he might just clip off the fire hydrant across the street before I'd get him stopped!

Smiling smugly to myself, Matt and I methodically annihilate Enemy from the driveway. And we turn to the sidewalks and backyard trails.

Cautiously we sneak around the corner of the garage, catching Enemy Snow completely by surprise. And with a full throttle of gas pumping into his pistons, he lunges forward, going for Enemy's soft underside.

Oh, but it's pretty as the stream of white shoots into the spruce trees, its final resting place for the winter. Then a smooth, snappy circle around the birdfeeders, sending black hulls of sunflower seeds flying amidst Enemy's innards.

And last, with victory at hand, along the path to Butch, my huntin' dog's kennel, Matthew and I slowly, casually swagger, savoring the sweetness of the moment, the defeat of the empire of Enemy Snow! Like as if we've just liberated Paris!

And I think I can hear music coming from one of the sidewalk cafes!

"I'm dreaming of a white New Year…" the words seem to be saying.

Matthew loves that song.

January, 1997

# Siberian Sled Dogs

They're a beautiful bunch! There they stood, all 15 of them, lined up against the wire fence of their kennel. There's Kayak, Klik, Kimik, Kulick, and more.

They're Siberian huskie sled dogs that Lamar and Pat Pockrandt keep at their secluded pine-log home deep in the pine woods north of Webb Lake in Burnett County, at Nooksack Kennels.

I'd come to visit with the Pockrandts, to learn about sled dog raising and sled dog racing. And the handsome animals were there to greet me, as I parked amongst the tall Norway pines. There, like a family portrait they posed, silent, their gray-white bodies still, their piercing pale blue eyes studying me.

I could almost read their minds. Who's this guy? What's he doing here, they seemed to be thinking.

Then, as I turned to walk the snow-lined trail to the house, in unison their voices sounded... a lyrical, musical, wolf-like howl that floated through the forest. A happy call, I decide, one that seems to flow from the bonds of kinship that binds the pack together.

Lamar welcomed me at the door. And as we adjourned to a study, Pat, who was busy with a winter project, greeted me.

"I was a horse-shoer, a farrier, all my life," Lamar began, "for thirty years in Minnesota. I'd always been around horses.

*Lamar Pockrandt readies his sled dogs for a fast run.*

I had a pony when I was four years old. I was used to doing
chores every day, and when I retired and we moved up here, I

missed that. So I bought a dog."

As time passed, more were added, all registered Siberian huskies. "Siberians are the pure breed," Lamar said. "The Alaskan huskie is a mixed breed that contains some Siberian."

Thus began a unique hobby and an unusual source of winter recreation for Pockrandt, the running of his dogs over trails that wind through the nearby jack pine forest, with Lamar riding a sled behind.

"The only racing I do is with myself," he said. "We average ten miles an hour. I have an odometer on the back of the sled. This year so far I have 630 miles on the dogs."

Pockrandt travels trails with big loops. "It's hard to turn the dogs on a trail," he said. "I run three days a week, except when there's fresh snow. That balls up on their feet, and I have to put booties on them which they don't like."

The dogs are transported in a truck with individual cages to the trail site. Pockrandt won't run the dogs out of his driveway because of the danger. Neither does he like trails with road crossings.

"I use voice commands," he said. " 'Gee' to go right, 'Haw' left, and 'Whoa' to stop. If we come to an intersection, the lead dog will look back at me for a command. Good lead dogs are worth a lot of money! All lead dogs are girl dogs. The boys will take off after squirrels!"

Caring for his dogs is a big job. "I feed at 4 pm," he explained. "Then they run on an empty stomach the next day. I feed a real good dog food and ground chicken, which I buy commercially. The dogs can lose fat and dehydrate, and this reduces that. I also feed a mix of electrolyte which makes the food more digestible and prevents lactic acid build-up in their muscles."

The dogs are kept in loose housing, males and females separate. "That way they take care of their own pecking order," he said. "They don't fight. They're happy when I hitch them together."

Snowmobiles are sometimes met on the trails. "I can hear them coming a quarter-mile away," Lamar said. "But they can't hear me. Some snowmobilers stop to talk. They really enjoy the dogs!"

Training begins after Labor Day with the dogs pulling Lamar on a four-wheel ATV until snow arrives. The sled season lasts usually to the first week in March when snow conditions begin to deteriorate.

Siberian huskies are bred to run. "They're real athletes!" Lamar said. "The first five miles of a run, you're absolutely out of control. You're going about 20 miles an hour. Then they settle down. They're like a battery that runs down. You have to give them rests to re-charge."

And later I went along as Pockrandt prepared for a run. I watched as, one by one, he hitched the eight dogs to their harnesses. I listened to their excited barking, as they impatiently waited to get going, the love for their sport showing in their eagerness.

Then, with a wave of his hand, Lamar signalled me off to the side as he lifted the snow hook that held the team. And in a blur of fur and a swirl of snow, they shot past me.

"See ya, Bob-b-b-b!" I heard Lamar call, his words growing faint as he and his dogs melted almost immediately into the distance.

Believe me, Lamar Pockrandt travels in some fast company!

Canine, that is.

February, 1996

# Of Oats And Oat Fields

A ride through the southern part of the state recently brought back some old memories. The harvest of oats was on. There the fields stood, golden-rich in the summer sun. Green-and-white self-propelled combines moved methodically along their edges, harvesting the crop.

Oats and oat fields were once big in my life, back in boyhood days. And the sight of the fields recalled thoughts of those times, of grandfathers, uncles, and a dad. And the work that went into bringing off a crop of oats, precious grain needed to feed cattle, horses, pigs and chickens in a winter that laid ahead.

Late February or early March, when the first rivlets of melted snow would drip from the barn eaves, always brought the first thoughts of oats. That's when my grandfather would dispatch a couple of his sons, my uncles, and me to the granary to get his seed oats ready for the coming spring planting.

My job was to turn the crank on the fanning mill, as my uncles shoveled in oats from a nearby bin. Through the mill, the shiny yellow grain would pass, coming out cleaned of chaff and weed seeds. One by one, tall gray canvas bags would be filled, tied with binder twine, and neatly stacked until Gramp announced that the supply would meet his needs.

As April approached, the black loam fields, plowed the fall before, would free themselves of snow, and gradually dry in the strengthening sun. Come a balmy morning, horses would be harnessed, hitched to discs, springtooths and drags, and the land prepared for planting.

When the dirt was smooth as talcum powder, Gramp would hitch his team to a high-wheeled grain drill and fill the hopper with the seed oats from the granary. Back and forth across the field he'd move, spreading the seed on the receptive earth, carefully following his wheel tracks to make sure there'd be no "skips." A farmer with "skips" in his oat fields got low marks on his farming report card in our neighborhood!

Late May and early June would bring the warm rains needed to germinate the seed, and seemingly overnight the fields would be clothed with a blush of lush green. Weeds would now capture the attention of my two grandfathers.

Both had a hatred for weeds… one for thistles, the other for yellow mustard. Let a patch of thistles appear, and I'd be dispatched with a hoe to do them in. Let a few sprigs of yellow mustard show their heads, and I'd get the job of pulling them. Many a day I stood hoeing in a hot sun! Many a mile I hiked across ankle-high oat fields!

With luck, by late July the fields would stand thick and tall with green stems waving before the summer breezes, tipped with lacy heads as the grain matured. Periodically Gramp would walk into the field, rub a handful of kernels in his palms, and smile if he liked what he saw.

Gradually, the green would fade to pale yellow as the crop ripened. And by mid-August, its golden glow told that harvest time had come. And best to get at it before a thunderstorm laid it flat!

Harvest time was exciting and action-packed, as I recall. Around the field, Gramp would move with a grain binder pulled by a three-horse team, the revolving reel of the binder laying the grain before the sharp sickle. Somehow the marvelous machine tied the grain with twine into bundles, sheaves that were collected on a carrier, then spit-out to the ground.

Following Gramp around the field would be his "shocking" crew: my uncles, me, even my aunts. Carrying a bundle under each arm, we'd build shocks of a dozen or so, standing the bundles upright, to shed the rain which hopefully wouldn't fall. Ah, but a field of freshly shocked oats looked pretty when we were done!

And finally "thrashing" time, that week or two when the big Case thresher, owned communally by the farmers in the neighborhood, would move from farm to farm to separate the oats from the straw.

Thrashing time for me meant driving teams of horses in the fields as the golden grain bundles were loaded and hauled to the churning thresher. And it meant a job at 50 cents a day as the "blower man" sitting atop the machine amidst spinning belts and pulleys, operating gears and ropes that guided the long pipe from which the straw spewed, building neat stacks of straw for my farmer employers.

And it meant long hours in bins alone, shoveling back the oats that flowed endlessly from the thresher. Dirty, dusty, dreary hours!

A feeling of relief always settled over our farm when thrashing was done. The oat crop was in again, safely stored in bins where, come winter, it would feed Gramp's livestock for another year.

Today, things have changed. The horses, the steel-wheeled wagons, the threshing machines, even the pitch forks are gone, replaced with modern technology that does the job.

What does remain, however, are memories... thoughts of a time when oats and oat fields were big in the life of a kid growing up in the country.

September, 1996